How To Get People To Do Things

How To Get People To Do Things

Robert Conklin

Contemporary Books, Inc.
Chicago

Library of Congress Cataloging in Publication Data

Conklin, Robert.
   How to get people to do things.

   1. Interpersonal relations.   2. Emotions.
3. Motivation (Psychology)   4. Persuasion
(Psychology)   I. Title.
HM132.C626   301.11   78-27021
ISBN 0-8092-7358-6

Copyright © 1979 by Robert Conklin
All rights reserved
Published by Contemporary Books, Inc.
180 North Michigan Avenue, Chicago, Illinois 60601
Manufactured in the United States of America
Library of Congress Catalog Card Number: 78-27021
International Standard Book Number: 0-8092-7358-6

Published simultaneously in Canada by
Beaverbooks, Ltd.
150 Lesmill Road
Don Mills, Ontario M3B 2T5
Canada

My heartfelt appreciation . . .

. . . to the many people in the organizations of which I am a part for their encouragement, faith, and endless efforts.

. . . to Personal Dynamics for the use of excerpts from the "Adventures in Attitudes" program.

Contents

How To Get People To Do Things

Prologue

We, the people in your life, want to talk with you about how you get along with us.

Our relationships are good. But we believe that by working together we can make them even better.

We're waiting to give you more love in the ways you'd like to be loved. You can make it easy for us to do that.

You could have a deeper effect on us, move us, motivate us to become greater than we have ever been before. Listen. We'll tell you how to do that.

Some of us don't know you yet, but we're looking forward to it. Let's make sure it happens.

Do you realize how anxious we are to help you be successful? We'll work hard at that if you'll just share a little more of yourself with us.

We know that you long to be needed and wanted. So do we. Shouldn't we be closer?

Do we seem to be holding back sometimes, hiding something

1

from you? We don't mean to. It's only that we are afraid of your reactions. Are we wrong?

Maybe we could be a little nicer to each other, more thoughtful, perhaps?

We're always responding to you, even in our silence. In fact, we're often communicating the most when we seem to be doing it the least.

At times we resist you, even get angry. But there are reasons for that. They should be brought out, made known. Are you ready to hear them?

Are we having enough fun together? Enjoying one another? Happy with each other? Just a thought.

We want to believe in you. But how do you feel about us?

Are you aware that we sense what you think about us, even though you try to hide those thoughts? That affects the way we get along with each other, you know.

We admit to causing you hurt and frustration at times. We can explain that, but we need your understanding.

What do you expect of us? We're very apt to be whatever that is.

Do you have any idea how important you are to us? We need your guidance, support, and trust. We usually ask for it in strange ways, don't we?

Some of us are very close to you, but there are some gaps, some empty places, that need filling in.

Maybe we're trying to do things *to* each other rather than *for* each other.

Let's make this relationship of ours really work. Let's grow.

Shouldn't we be thinking about these things?

Let's get started!

1

Why People Will Give You
What You Want

"So, to the degree you give others what they want, they will give you what you want."

It was Bill Stilwell from the Management Institute, University of Wisconsin, summing up a two-day conference on motivation and persuasion.

I seized a pencil and wrote down his statement. It was one of those rare, precious, profound chunks of insight that can change the course of one's existence.

I wished I had learned its meaning years before.

To the degree you give others what they want, they will give you what you want!

That is the key to persuading, leading, motivating, selling, supervising, influencing, guiding others—getting people to do things for you.

You can read all the books, take all the courses, spend thousands of hours pursuing the secrets of affecting the thoughts and behavior of others, and you will discover it can all be compressed into that one sentence.

To the degree you give others what they want, they will give you what you want!

It seems incredibly simple. Perhaps it is, if you really understand it. But few do. For there are some implications of the rule that you must know and apply before you can make it work for you. Otherwise, the principle seems to work in reverse: People resist you, act against you, do the things you do not want them to do.

For instance, you must *first* give others what they want. Then they give you the things you want. Most people have that twisted around.

A man says to himself, "I would give my wife a box of candy if she would show me more affection."

An employer feels that an employee should get praise and recognition after putting forth some extra effort.

"I'll start having confidence in my kids when they get some decent grades in school," mutters a parent.

"I could be a lot warmer toward George if he weren't so cold and grouchy," Maude silently thinks.

A salesperson tells a manager, "Wow! Would I ever be excited if I cracked the Flanex account!"

These people have the formula backward.

The man has to bring his wife the candy *first;* then he will get more affection.

The employer must give praise and recognition *first* in order to bring forth the extra effort from the employee.

The parent has to express confidence in the kids *first;* then they will start coming through with better grades.

Maude has to warm up to George *first;* then the indifference and grumpiness of George will melt away.

The salesperson must generate excitement *first;* then the big, juicy sales will fall into place.

So that's the way the law works. You *first* give others what they want; then they will give you what you want.

Of course, it takes patience. And a few other things.

Like knowing *what* it is people want. (We'll get to that later.)

And knowing *how* to give them the things they want. (We'll get to that later, too.) And knowing what it is *you* want and what you're willing to give in order to get it. We'll get to that right now.

Because if you want to manipulate and shuffle people around for your own satisfaction, if you want to inflate your own ego by gaining power over those who are vulnerable, if you are looking for tricky ways to maneuver people into buying things they don't need, if you feel the need to dominate or subdue others (perhaps even your own family) and are looking for psychological buttons to push to always get your own way . . . then you are reading the wrong book.

For in spite of the title, this is not a book about getting; it's about giving. And loving. And succeeding. In fact, it's about becoming immensely successful. For if you can get things done with people in joy and harmony, helping them grow and become more than they ever have been before, then you have one of the most treasured talents anyone can possess. The world needs you. It is waiting to reward you highly in material or emotional benefits, to give *you* the things *you* want.

PEOPLE GO IN THE WRONG DIRECTIONS

With a pathway so open and available, why don't more people get on it to go where they want to go? It's probably because of a fork in the road. People are going to go in one of two directions. They are going to be concerned only with what they want or else with what others want. One or the other. Their wants or those of others. Many are so blinded by their personal wants that they give very little thought to filling the needs of others.

Mary knows what she wants from her husband, but what he wants never fully gets through to her.

The foreman knows he wants those lug bolts tightened as the body frame comes through the assembly line, but what does the one doing the tightening want?

The parents know the way they want their children to grow

up, but do they show as much concern for what the children want (emotionally, that is)?

The salesperson has a strong desire to sell the stove but is almost afraid to ask about the prospect's wants, for fear the product won't fit.

Paul feels that Jane does not love him the way he wants to be loved. Maybe it's because he has been blind to her wants and needs.

The teacher wants that dull, sleepy-eyed teenager to be more attentive, but what does the gawky young stalk of humanity want? Has enough regard been invested in that?

And so it goes. Everyone wants something from someone else and becomes frustrated when it is not forthcoming.

Do you know what often happens then? They start applying an upside-down version of the rule. They try punishing people, just what people do *not* want, in an effort to get what they want.

The air gets chilly when Mary doesn't get what she wants from Frank. The foreman chews out the lug bolt tightener. The parents scold, spank, and threaten when the children do not fit the mold. The salesperson jabbers on desperately when it appears the prospect is lukewarm. "Maybe Jane will shape up if I make her a little jealous," Paul reasons. And the teacher threatens, shames, and disciplines, in futile attempts to shake off the teenager's lethargy.

So that's the story of the human being in a highly individualized society. Divorces, splits in families, high job turnover, heavy hearts, wasted careers, crumbled dreams, lonely lives—all haunted by ineffective efforts to relate to other people.

Find out what people want.

Then help them get it.

That's the way to reverse most of those distressing situations!

It's another way of describing the rule. Or the first part of it, that is: "To the degree you give others what they want. . . ."

CHANGE "WANT" TO "NEED"

I have observed this process functioning successfully for a

number of years. I am more dedicated to it and enthusiastic about it now than when I first heard it. The joys of my personal life have flowered from the use of it. The barren, rocky moments have resulted when my emotions got in the way of my using the rule.

I would make only one change in the formula. Replace the word *want* with *need.*

Wants and needs are separate substances. Wants are frivolous, itchy, plundering, often greedy forces that are never satisfied. Meet one want, and there are two more to replace it.

But needs are the deeper currents of one's existence. They are meaningful, worthy, and not as capricious as wants.

People want sympathy; they need empathy.

People want riches; they need fulfillment.

People want big cars and expensive homes; they need transportation and shelter.

People want fame; they need recognition.

People want power; they need support and cooperation.

People want to dominate; they need to influence and guide.

People want prestige; they need respect.

Children want freedom and permissiveness; they need discipline.

People want make-believe relationships; they need honesty and reality.

People want ease and comfort; they need achievement and work.

People want adoration; they need love.

So let's say, "To the degree you give others what they need, they will give you what you need."

Let's think about that. What do people really need? What do you and I really need? To discover that, we must become rather close. But we can do that.

For there are few relationships more intimate than that of author and reader. The relationship is silent—no verbal interruptions, no detours. It's a very private conversation between two people, never more. The author, if sincere, is speaking from the heart in a way most understandable to the reader. The reader can reject, accept, pause, ponder, reread, react in any way he or she chooses, without any of the risks accompanying other types of communication.

It's a warm and wonderful association. I, for one, am going to enjoy every word of it. I hope you do, too. I would like to be your friend. That means I must open up and disclose myself to you. When I do that, you will not only know me, but you will also get to know yourself a lot better. And others. This is called "relating."

That's how you will discover what others need so that you can apply our formula: "To the degree you give others what they need, they will give you what you need." Relate. Open up. Remove your mask, and others will remove theirs.

KNOWING ME IS KNOWING YOU

Let me remove my mask. You will see what I mean. For as I talk of myself and the things I need, you will discover that I am also talking about you and the things you need. I'll begin by saying:

"Love me!

"Give me someone, as I wander through life, who cares about me—someone who picks me out of the crowd, notices me, remembers me, makes me believe I'm special."

This is the plea churning about within every human being. It is the greatest hunger of life.

Love is the mainspring of the heart. It is the meaning, the joy, the valleys and the mountains of being.

Love freshens the body, nourishes the soul, shapes the spirit, and glorifies the mind. It is the laughter of the heart, the sunrise of each moment.

Above all else, love is an emotion. That's why it is so vital to the pulse of life. For people are emotional beings. Everything they do is shaped by their emotions.

I wish I could tell you more about emotions, classify them, establish them in the order of their intensity, and find words to make them completely understandable. But that would be a little like trying to describe what a mushroom tastes like. It is impossible.

I only know about *my* feelings. Not yours. We can never know exactly how another person feels. I can laugh with you in your laughter, cry with you in your sorrow, rejoice with you in your happiness, or fret with you in your despair. That is empathy. But neither of us can feel exactly the same way the other feels.

Only you know about your feelings. And only I know about mine. And neither of us are even too clear about that.

But if we can talk to each other about our inner selves, we'll be able to compare, understand, and accept who we are significantly better. And that will help us in getting along with each other—and the people close to us.

So I'll tell you about my feelings, and maybe that will aid you to see yours more clearly.

WE NEVER REALLY GROW UP

A large part of my emotional direction was established very early in life. The longer I live, the more impressed I am about that. Now that I am a seasoned adult, it seems I should have outgrown my childhood nature. But I haven't. I know now I won't.

My childhood was a struggle to receive friendship, acceptance, love and recognition. Just like chickens, a pecking order was established in the flock of children. Who was the smartest, funniest, strongest, cutest, or most popular? Who could run the fastest, throw a stone the farthest, hold their breath the longest, or win the most marbles?

I sure didn't end up on top. But the great mass of other kids were there with me, reacting about as I did. At that age one doesn't talk about feelings of inadequacy or inferiority. So at times it seemed as though I were alone, separated from the whole world.

Like striking an already bruised muscle, criticism, rejection, failure, or rebuke intensified this conviction. I would not let this be found out, because it seemed shameful, a sign of weakness—

proof, perhaps, that I didn't deserve to be on the top of the heap.

I hung on dearly to every indication of love or recognition. Like the comment of Jennie Murphy, my eighth-grade English teacher, who suggested I could write.

"You're a little like Abraham Lincoln," she said. "You say a lot in a few words." A moment later she revealed that she knew I was one of the boys who had tipped over her outhouse on Halloween. What a magnificent person! She was the only teacher throughout my sixteen years of school who said anything good about my academic ability.

Little wonder that at times I had a complex about being a bit backward and dumb, without question quite average intellectually.

I suppose the acorn never stops needing the earth, the moisture, and the air, even after it becomes a grown tree. So, here I am, an adult, and find I have changed so very little in my needs since those long-ago days.

I still seek recognition and acceptance.

I still flourish with praise and crumble with criticism and rejection.

At times I still feel lonely—not when I'm alone or with someone I know well, but when I am surrounded by strangers. In a crowded shopping center, for instance, I feel awkward, distant from everyone else. People stare at me not as a human being, it seems, but as a thing. I want a friendly face to look into, want to meet eyes that say "Hello" rather than "Don't come near me." Perhaps that is why a warm welcome and a smile is so pleasing from one who serves me in a store. It relieves, for a moment, a loneliness.

There are short spaces when I have a strong yearning to be loved. I do not mean physical love, although that is important. I refer to the communication of emotional love. These spans of longing usually come after I have been heavily involved with people for long periods of time. It is almost like wanting a recess, a coffee break, a point of surrender from the process of living. I want to know that all the effort, the trying to be loved, gets some results. I must go to someone who cares about me and merely be in that person's presence quietly and effortlessly and be fulfilled with the sense of being loved.

So I have found that most of the things I want from living I must get from people. It would simplify life to be able to say that I don't need others, that I can exist only with my God, my work, running in the morning, paddling my canoe among the water lilies in the bay, looking at mountain peaks, or just being alone.

I enjoy those things deeply and peacefully, but my life would be shallow if that were all I had. I want to tell someone about my experiences. I must share myself with people.

I have much yet to accomplish with my life. This requires the help of others. I need people to notice me, encourage me, accept me, praise me, and care about me.

You might say, "But you have all of those. Don't you know that?"

And I would respond, "Yes, I know that, logically. You've been around a long time, so I know you are my friend. You married me, you work with me, you fill my car with gas, or you play golf with me. So I know you must be my friend.

"But I do not know it emotionally unless you communicate it and I experience it. If you love me, touch me. If you like being with me, smile at me. If you miss me, write to me. Then my feelings as well as my mind will know of our love and friendship. You will be helping me. For the energy of my life is my emotion. That is the substance that stimulates me to achieve, grow, work, progress, and become more than I was yesterday.

"And when you do this for me, then I'm a little like a puppy dog. Stroke me, show me affection, and I'll wag my tail, jump up and down, follow you around, and do the things you ask me to do. But your strokes and affection must be real. For, like the little dog, I can tell if it is. If your attention is a false device to manipulate me, I'll find you out and resist you."

ARE WE SIMILAR?

It is not easy for me to disclose myself this way. We are alike, you and I, in that respect. We hide our real selves from the world. We keep our insecurities, doubts, weaknesses, and needs under cover. Perhaps we are saying, "I don't want you to give me the things I need because I have asked for them. I don't want your pity and charity. I want your love and respect." So we conceal our deepest longings, making sure we earn that which we hope for from others. Maybe that's all right. At any rate, that's the way it is.

So why do I bother going through this unnatural process?

Because I don't believe you are very much different from me. We may have traveled separate paths to get this way. Our emotional temperatures might vary. But beneath the surface we are really quite alike.

We yearn to be needed, wanted, and loved. We want to be important to someone. We need appreciation, satisfaction, recognition, acceptance, fulfillment, and a whole lot of other things that we reach out for from within.

Most others are like you and me. Remember, to the degree you give others what they need, they will give you what you need.

What do others need? Look well within yourself, and you will find that which exists in others. What you need, they need. What is closest to your heart, emotionally, is also closest to theirs. You are your own barometer, your own measuring device, of what you need to give in order to get what you need from life.

YOU TAKE OUT WHAT YOU PUT IN

You now have the key for getting people to do things for you. It's simple, isn't it? That's as it should be. It resembles the natural course of life. You were born into a sea of life, existing in harmony with all others. You usually do things best when you do them with others, in cooperation, mutual trust, joy, and satisfaction.

The principles are so easy that a child can use them. Regardless of your personality, you have the capacity to get along better with people—but only by giving and sharing of yourself.

This calls to mind the man in a desolate mountain region who was a laborer six days a week and a preacher on the seventh. He served a small rural congregation tucked far up in the hills. The only monetary compensation he got came from the morning offering. One Sunday his six-year-old daughter went along with him to the service. Just inside the door of the small frame church was a table, and on it rested a collection basket. As they entered, the daughter saw her father place a half-dollar in the wicker basket before any of the people arrived.

When the service had ended and the last member had departed, the parson and his daughter started to leave. As they reached the door, both peered expectantly into the collection basket and found that the only "take" was the half-dollar he had donated.

After a short silence the little girl said, "You know, Daddy, if you had put more in, you'd have gotten more out!"

2

How to Make Love

If you have a relationship that has some sour overtones to it, there are only three ways to make it sweeter. In other words, only three possible solutions exist for "people problems."

That should catch your attention. Because it covers quite a chunk of life that makes you turn up red eyeballs—worries and frustrations caused by your kids, marriage partners, boss, neighbors, roommate, nosy acquaintances, and the bullies that shove in front of you at the checkout counter.

Here are the three choices:

1. Change the situation
2. Change the person
3. Change yourself

Let's consider each one, starting with the first: Change the situation. If you don't like the boss, quit your job. If your spouse causes hurricanes to rage in your head instead of making harps play in your heart, then dump him or her. If getting along with your teacher is like clawing through a jungle of barbed wire, then drop out of school. Or if Mom and Pop are always on your back, then hit the streets. Run away from home.

That's to say that if the association with another person has bad rumbles, break out, split, disappear. That could be the best solution in some cases. Maybe. But there are deeper considerations. Such as, what are the consequences? What are you doing to yourself?

I had lunch with Jim Beattie. He's the executive director of Nexus, a therapeutic center for rehabilitating young felons. These felons come to Jim's place with an average of ten arrests each and eleven long months spent in juvenile correctional institutions.

"All these kids know how to do when they have a bad human encounter is to act crazy and run away," Jim told me. "After they're with us awhile, they realize how dumb that is. Running away doesn't work."

Another time a friend was talking to me about his divorce. "We found that marriage was different than going together. Little things became big things. We got real good at making each other miserable. Every day was a drag. So we split. It wasn't easy, but we did it.

"Life, I thought, would be all rosy after that. There would be no more tears and hassles. Life would be a lark! Ah, sweet freedom!

"But it wasn't quite that way. What I thought would be freedom was prolonged remorse. I couldn't get rid of the feelings of guilt and shame and a sense of failure. I knew those were a separate set of problems that should have been dealt with differently. But there was a gut feeling chewing away inside, telling me that happiness is not built by messing up someone else's life.

"Do I still hold myself responsible? Of course not. I've put it behind me now. But I learned that solving bad scenes with others doesn't always mean breaking off. For me it didn't do much for the real problem. It was me. I took that right along with me. Maybe the outcome would be the same today. I don't know. I'd deal with it a lot differently."

A woman once told me how she'd skipped from job to job, trying to find the right situation.

"People got to me," she said. "Criticism, complaints, moaning, groaning—it seemed that's all I heard all day. I couldn't get it off my mind at night. So I kept moving, only to find out the names and faces changed, but not the humans. Most of the old frustrations would come up again, just dressed differently.

"So it finally dawned on me that the problem was me, not them. I'm doing something about that now. I think I'm going to make it."

Does this mean that a divorce or change of jobs should be ruled out as a way out of unhappy attachments? No. You have to decide what's best for you. All you're getting here are some insights and ideas to use for guidelines. Running away might be the easiest answer but not the best. If you've got a marriage, job, or friendship that has some good parts to it, then consider another option for smoothing out the rough spots.

MOST PEOPLE WANT TO CHANGE OTHERS

Here's the second solution: Change the other person. That's the one that holds the greatest appeal from most people's viewpoint. Much of what I hear indicates that by instinct and impulse people are always trying to solve their own problems by changing others.

"He had better be straightened out!"

"You could try to be a little more thoughtful."

"How do you get the message through to these teenagers?"

"She's simply got to change her attitude. That's all there is to it."

"How do you motivate people?"

"I just can't put up with you acting that way anymore."

"Will you please listen to me and do as I say?"

"Don't jazz around with 'em. Get 'em in line!"

Sooooo . . . It gets to be a little overwhelming at times, doesn't it? The only way out is to get people to change.

I used to think so. I spent many years trying to make it work. I still do at times. Dumb me. Because generally it doesn't work.

In the work environment I've put in hours, days, even months, I guess, trying to change people. Most of them do change, a little. Or they just act somewhat better for a short period of time. Then they slip back into the old pattern. Or they console me by being what I want when they're around me. But only then. Away from me, they relax and be what they feel most comfortable being.

Or my attempt to change them sort of dullens them. It's like giving people a tranquilizer called "confusion." It settles into their nervous system and deadens the naturalness and sparkle, the effervescence of the spirit.

DO PEOPLE CHANGE EASILY?

Stop and think, for a moment, how people act when you try to change them. First, you have a leakproof case built up before you even propose change. That's easy. Human beings are so vulnerable, with such a variety of weaknesses and defects, that they are almost totally defenseless when approached with an argument for change.

The time for confrontation arrives. You make the presentation. Or, if it isn't done like that, the attempts at change are administered in little doses over extended periods of time. That's called nagging.

The reactions are unpredictable. At times appreciation may be feigned. "Just what I needed," comes out. But not usually.

More often there's a trembling effort to explain, justify, hold on to what they are. That's natural. Remember, you're penetrating people's defenses and they need those, so they'll hang on. Strip one of one's defenses and you'll end up with fluff—nothing. A person will fall apart.

So they'll protect themselves by logic, anger, blame, rationalization, stony silence, or intimidated departure. Perchance you've had a positive effect. Probably not.

Go through this process with someone who really cares about you, and the reaction could be more somber. If the affection is honest, the person is going to be more likely to change. That doesn't indicate weakness, but a willingness to drop off any traits that make you unhappy.

First comes the heart-to-heart talk, usually disguised as a chat, to uplift the togetherness. Soon the face becomes clouded. Emotions might be bruised. Tears, words, and old wounds surface. Let's assume you win your point. It's a little like defeating an adversary.

For the next few days the other one will spend more time alone, apart from you. You'll be treated nicely but quietly. There's a strained expression on the face, reflecting an inner concern about being wrong.

That's the way people are when you convince them that they should not like themselves the way they are.

Is that any kind of a solution for a human relations problem? Because you have power over another because of love, appointed position, or some other power, should that be used to impose one's will on another? I think not. At least it hasn't worked for me.

Think about it for yourself. Would the imposition of another's will on yourself make you feel better about yourself? Would it make the relationship richer, finer, deeper, more powerful in a meaningful direction? What does it do to the other person?

If you come to the same conclusions I have, then, alas! Only one solution remains for solving people problems.

Change yourself!

That's tough to do sometimes. Not sometimes, almost always. Really uphill.

What makes it difficult, you see, is that you're right and the other person is inexcusably wrong. I don't mean that jokingly. I'm serious.

Think back to the last argument or difference of opinion that you had with someone close to you, even your employers. Who was right? You were, weren't you? And, furthermore, you could win a case before the Supreme Court, God, and ten thousand others with your own conscience proving your point.

In fact, during your lifetime how many skirmishes with others have you had that were your fault? Aren't most of your major and minor miseries in life caused by others?

What have been your reactions as other people tried to rewrite your personal scripts, tried to change you? Did you come out with, "That's a lovely idea! I'll start right away . . . "? In rare instances, possibly. In all likelihood, however, you defended what you did or were.

You'll change, feel better, as soon as others change. Ever have that feeling? That's what makes changing so thorny. Since you've been right all along, why should you change?

There's really only one answer to that. It is by far the best way, in almost every instance, for removing the abrasions from your life. Others change when you change. You act, people react.

Most interpersonal problems stem from everybody's attempt to get everybody else to change. It starts early in life and goes on and on:

"Why don't you . . . ?"
"You should have. . . ."
"How come you . . . ?"
"If you'd only. . . ."
"You ought to. . . ."

There is nothing wrong with the words per se, except that they usually end up as a criticism, a put-down. People don't like to be put down. So they get angry, fight back.

That's the best reason for you to do the changing. It stands out as a starting point, a magic key, for the conflicts with others.

WHY SHOULD YOU BE THE ONE TO CHANGE?

You say, "Hey! It isn't fair that I always have to change myself to make my relationships better."

And I'll answer, "You've got it right, my friend. It isn't fair." There are a lot of crusades going on to support that. We can get into liberation, discrimination, persecution, sex hostility, prejudice, and be-yourself causes that preach beyond a smidgen of a doubt that others should change to make your life better, not you.

About all I have to offer to counter that is that changing yourself works better than trying to change others. It will make your life better. You'll move ahead faster and further than you ever thought possible. Good relationships become even better. Fouled up circumstances unsnarl. Life gets wider and wider instead of narrower and narrower.

It doesn't work every time. Nothing does. But it's worth a try before you spend a lot of time groping around, trying to make the first two solutions to "people problems" prove out.

It'll shake up the jowls of your disposition, put a strain on the muscles of your temperament. But getting started, struggling off dead center, will get you moving. It will be easier and easier as you go along.

Here's one for you to try. The next time your spouse gets tired and owly and cuts you short or snaps your neck a little, smile, look back, and say, "I love you." Not a sarcastic, "I love you, too, sourpuss." But a soft, sincere, "I love you," just a shade above a whisper. Try it. I promise it won't hurt a bit. The results might amaze you.

When you're criticized or put down, smile and say something like, "Thanks for letting me know." Try it on for size once or twice just to see if it fits, making sure you smile.

IT'S IMPORTANT TO SMILE

"We've done some research with videotape, filming people in normal conversation," said Professor James McConnell, a psychologist at the University of Michigan. "Most people are surprised how infrequently they smile."

He advised that smiling can help you do better at your job, be a more effective parent, and enjoy life more. He reports that frowning physicians face twice as many malpractice suits as smiling doctors. One study revealed that eighty percent of the parents of juvenile delinquents were habitual nonsmilers.

Some research done on the West Coast showed that men smiled at only twelve percent of other men. But they smiled at seventy percent of the women! Department store sales have gone up as much as twenty percent when salespeople have gone on a smiling campaign! Smile! Smile! Smile! It's a delightful way to change.

Try agreeing with people instead of disagreeing with them. See how right you can make others instead of how wrong. Just for thirty days. Your world won't come apart in that short time. And you might find out some things about yourself that are worth knowing.

WHERE CHANGING YOURSELF STARTS

All this business of changing yourself starts somewhere that's very tender. It's tucked away deep inside, but you've got to get to it if you're going to make any honest changes in the way you relate to others.

It's your attitude, the way you think about the people in your life. Before you can turn your head and heart around, there's a substance called "forgiving" that must be spawned. That's how changing yourself starts.

"What do you mean?" you ask. "Who do I have to forgive?" I'm with you, my friend. I used to think the same way.

But now I'd answer, "Just about anyone who has ever ruffled your feathers."

A long time ago, when I was a sales manager in a small company, I found out that a fellow in the office was having a secret affair with my secretary. Both were married.

In a way I felt betrayed. What they were doing was not right. So, in a nebulous manner, I felt that I was attached to their wrongdoing. I had to redeem myself, restore morality, maybe even get a sugar cube of vengeance.

I confronted the fellow in front of his manager. I had him dead. I knew it. He knew it. He stuttered, stammered, turned red, squirmed, and I did nothing except bore in a little harder.

Both of the people involved resigned. I reasoned that I was dealing with the situation in the best interests of the company. I felt satisfied, righteous. I shouldn't have. It was an indecent, brutish way of acting.

But that was years ago. I didn't know much about forgiving. I thought that forgivingness was a virtue for which one received a bit of glory without having to give up too much in return. I could forgive a person, for example, if that person disagreed with me, admitted it, and asked my forgiveness. Or if someone called me a name during a heated argument, then apologized and asked to be forgiven, I could rise to my most noble nature and grant forgiveness, rather like a king pardoning a subject.

But now, years later, I believe that forgivingness is a quality of considerable consequence. It is a process of picking off thistles on the mind, which is not always effortless. For, in some cases, the roots have grown deep.

One of the most famous short stories ever written deals with this. Guy de Maupassant's masterpiece *A Piece of String* tells of a Norman peasant, Maître Hauchecorne, who could not forgive.

The thirty-year-old man was walking through the bustling marketplace one day when he saw a piece of string on the ground. He stooped down, picked up the string, and put it in his pocket. He was seen doing it and was accused later of having found a wallet lost at about the same spot.

He protested vigorously but was nevertheless taken to the local police station. He displayed his piece of string but was still not believed.

The next day the lost wallet was found. The episode was forgotten. To all, that is, except Maître Hauchecorne. He kept brooding about the injustice of being falsely accused. To everyone he met he complained of the manner in which he had been insulted.

The piece of string became the sole occupant of his mind. His farm was neglected The venom of self-pity slowly destroyed him. Unable to forgive, the old peasant died of a broken heart, after complaining to the very end about the piece of string.

Research indicates that the story could very well be based on fact. According to one report, the surging devastation of harbored resentment and hatred can actually kill a person. Not being able to "forgive and forget" causes the blood to clot more quickly, blood cells to increase, and stomach muscles to squeeze down and inhibit the digestive process. The overpowering effect of this intense emotion has been known to cause a stroke or heart attack.

We don't need burdens like that to carry around, do we? Far better that we learn to forgive than to burden ourselves with such dismaying loads.

THE "GIVING" OF FORGIVING

How does one forgive? A friend laid that on me once. You aren't going to like what he said. "Forgiveness always starts," he explained, "by your asking the other person to forgive you."

Are you ready for that? I wasn't. But when you turn it over a couple of times, it begins to make sense.

Whenever you have to forgive someone else for something, there is usually some malice, vindictiveness, bitterness, blame, or fault-finding sticking to the walls of your own mind. That might be what needs to be forgiven. Think about it.

Of one thing we can be certain. As long as you're forgiving, be sure to forgive yourself. Don't be too harsh on you. If you're wiping the slate clean with others, why not yourself? You can't feel good about others unless you feel good about you.

Another certainty—giving is the critical part of forgiving. You have to give to forgive. Forgiving always means surrendering a part of yourself, even if it is merely a black little thought that is throwing shadows across your feelings for another.

That takes humility, the kind possessed by Dr. Charles Mayo, who, with his brother, Will, founded the world-famous Mayo Clinic.

Dr. Charlie, as he was called, once entertained an English

visitor in his home at Rochester, Minnesota, for several days. At night the visitor put his shoes outside the door, expecting a servant to shine them. Dr. Charlie shined them himself. That's giving.

There is a Jewish story of two brothers whose farms lay side by side. One night, after the gathering of the harvest, the elder brother said to his wife: "My brother is a lonely man who has neither wife nor children. I will carry some of my sheaves into his field." But to his amazement, the next morning his stack of grain was as large as before. He continued to carry part of his harvest to his brother's farm each night, but every morning his own store of grain seemed untouched. The mystery was not revealed until one moonlit night the brothers, with their arms full of sheaves, met midway, face to face! Because of the generosity shown by the brothers, on this spot a temple was built, for the neighbors considered it to be the place where earth was nearest to heaven.

Glenn Cunningham was a miler whose legs had been burned so badly when he was a boy that the doctors said he would never walk. He ended up winning an Olympic gold medal, then devoted his life to helping troubled kids. He told me that his wife asked once, "Glenn, why do we have to give so much more than others? No one else is doing what we are."

"That's the reason, Ruth. No one else is doing it," he replied.

That could be why there are so many fouled up relationships in the world. No one is doing what they have to do to get them untangled. Forgiving.

You know what we're getting to here, don't you? Something that's akin to forgiving.

That's loving.

It's what this book is about. Loving.

HOW TO MAKE LOVE

There has been a lot preached and written about love but not enough on how to do it. It seemed right to do a book on "how to make love." We don't see enough of that today. People are trying to make their lives work without it and are coming up barren. Many are being misguided by what they read and hear.

There are those, for instance, who suggest that something other than love will get you what you want from others. Not true. Love is the only mechanism that is really effective in winning people's cooperation.

Some say sex without love is OK. It doesn't work out in the long run. Sex should be the blossom of a relationship, not the root.

Some mistake affection for love. They hug and kiss and talk about love, trying to get turned on by people in general. But no rockets are going off inside, except when they're with a few people with whom they have very close relationships. There's a lot of empty places that aren't filled. Why? Because they're going at love the wrong way. Affection can be a part of loving, but it's not love.

Most believe that love is an emotion. That's the illusion that keeps them from loving. For they hear of all the lovely thoughts and beautiful things that happen when you feel love. So they look to others for emotional highs so those wonderful things will happen to them. There's a hollowness as they end up short.

LOVING IS THINKING AND DOING

The emotional feeling that is called love, you see, is merely the reward for loving.

Loving is thinking and doing. It starts out as an attitude and ends up as an emotion. Many try to reverse this. They wait around for the emotion, expecting their minds to be filled with exotic thoughts. It seldom happens.

Love is an ability, an attitude. In fact, love is little less than life itself lived in the right way, with others. It is helping rather than hurting. Anyone can love. It starts with a concern, a sensitivity to others, and grows from there.

The capacity for loving is infinite. It expands as one lives—but only if it becomes stronger by thinking and doing.

The thinking comes from loving everything and everybody.

Rise above the pettiness, resentment, judgment, and prejudice. Just love.

Then do. That need not be big things. Just a lot of little everyday acts will be fine! Speak love. Ah, yes! Make love with your voice. These are the sounds of love:

"Let me help you."

"Excuse me."

"That's nice."

"I'll do it."

"I like you."

"Is that too much trouble?"

"Please."

"You'll like this better."

"Use mine."

"Tell me about your trip."

"Are you comfortable?"

"I'll wait for you."

"Thank you."

"I thought about you."

"That's a new coat!"

"You're fun to have around."

"Pardon me."

"This flower is for you."

"Have a good time!"

"It's up to you."

That's a proper place to stop. It's up to you how much you love. It shouldn't depend on how much you're loved. The music of your life is written by the warmth of your love, by what you think and do.

Love. It's the one thing that infallibly works to make your life richer, deeper, higher, wider—filled with emotional joy and satisfaction.

All of this is just another way of saying:

"To the degree that you give others what they need they will give you what you need!"

3

Appeal to the Deepest Craving of Human Nature

The mother and her fourteen-year-old son were having a discussion about his first girlfriend.

"What does she like about you?" Mom asked.

"That's easy," he said. "She thinks I'm handsome, fun, smart, talented, a good dancer."

What do you like about her?"

"That she thinks I'm handsome, fun, smart, talented, a good dancer."

That's the way the flower blossoms—toward the sunshine! The sunshine of your life is the person who makes you feel important, good about yourself. You are attracted to those people in whose presence you can say, "I like myself better when I'm with you!"

One of the most deeply rooted and compelling motivations that you have is the need to like yourself. If the concept of yourself that you carry around is acceptable to you, then life will soar like a lark on a spring day. But if you don't like yourself, the days and years will be quite a struggle; after all, being with someone you dislike for twenty-four hours a day is an awful barrier to a happy existence.

Love is so powerful because being loved causes one to love oneself. Nothing contributes to the self-image more than being loved by another. When the words "I love you" are expressed to you for the first time by another, your world blossoms; your heart glows with inspiration, confidence, and thoughts of the mountains you can move. It's more than an emotional kick; suddenly you like yourself more than you ever have before.

PEOPLE HELP YOU LIKE YOURSELF

Your self-image, the way you think of yourself, changes according to the situations and circumstances you're in and people you're with. Yes, people can have an enormous influence on your self-image. For people build up or tear down; they cause joy or hurt; they give confidence or doubt. In some people's presence you feel poised, able, and self-assured. You suddenly become elected president of the world! Those splendid individuals have the precious ability to make you like yourself in an expanded dimension.

On the other hand there are those who cause your self-concept to wilt and wrinkle with their caustic remarks, criticism, indifference, put-downs, or overwhelming successes compared with yours. Those are the ones who depress and discourage you; in their presence your efforts diminish, your adequacy shrinks; you feebly fight back with antagonism, lethargy, or disinterest. You have stopped liking yourself; your defenses are stripped and you want desperately to get back at those who caused this.

CRITICISM MAY BE HARMFUL

Unfortunately, too many close relationships are fraught with this critical process. This, to some extent, accounts for the success of the computer in helping children to learn. The computer never criticizes.

William Glasser, a psychiatrist who originated Reality Therapy and parental guidance programs, believes that "criticizing children is the most destructive thing you can do." Asking a child, "Why did you spill the milk?" is, he says, like most critical remarks, generally useless except that it drives the youngster into a shell.

A friend of mine, Jay Beecroft, is director of training for a large American corporation that employs more than ninety thousand people. At breakfast one day, Jay described a new concept in training his staff had developed. "We call it our positive reinforcement program," he explained. "We have come to realize that almost all of our training up to now has been of a critical nature. We have also arrived at the conclusion that there is no such thing as 'constructive criticism.' Criticism is destructive. It does not make people feel better about themselves."

Their "positive reinforcement" approach is a process of looking for the good qualities of individuals. Supervisory personnel emphasize the positive characteristics of employees.

Results, as Jay described them, have been dramatic. Absenteeism in those plants using the program has decreased over three percent. Not much, you might think, until you find out that each percentage point means sixty thousand dollars in savings to the company annually!

The program was implemented by trainers in the three lowest sales branches of one division. Two years later the sales volumes of those branches had risen from the lowest in the division to the highest.

So performance is remarkably more effective when people are encouraged to think well of themselves instead of being reminded of their shortcomings.

YOU NEED TO FEEL IMPORTANT

These people are no different from you. You, too, have an ever-present little person within you that wants to be made to feel important. It's your alter ego, your self-image. You are attracted to the person who contributes to your positive self-image. You feel a bond with that type of individual. You want to love, live with, work for, buy from, and do things for the special people who cause you to value yourself.

Every other human being is essentially like you. And that's the key to getting others to do things for you. Remember? To the degree that you give others what they need, they are going to give you what you need. People need to leave you saying, "I like myself better when I'm with you."

Many stories are told about the legendary coach of the Green Bay Packer football team, Vince Lombardi. One described an incident when he was seriously ill in a Washington, D.C., hospital. Willie Davis, the former all-pro defensive end for Green Bay, got on a plane in Los Angeles, flew to Washington, visited with Lombardi for only a couple minutes, and then flew back home.

"I had to go," Davis explained. "I just had to. That man made me feel I was important." There is an almost uncontrollable urge to do things for the person who makes one feel important. It's an outcropping of the deeply imbedded hunger to accept and like oneself.

It has been estimated that as much as ninety percent of the things we do are prompted by a desire to feel important. Unfortunately, most of a person's experiences while growing up are identified with losing, failing, being woefully inadequate.

LOOK FOR THE GOOD QUALITIES IN OTHERS

The kids call Peggy "Fatty." The teacher tells her she's lazy, capable of much better work. Her mother nags her about her sloppy appearance. She doesn't go to school dances, because she knows she won't be asked to dance. She gets laughed at in gym class because she's awkward and slow. Peggy wants to study arts and crafts; her Dad bugs her to take typing and shorthand. She manages to get through the blemishes on the face and the braces on the teeth, and she grows up.

Now you come along. You look past the shyness, the pounds on the hips, the spectacles, and the misshapen nose. You become a lot of people to Peggy, the people she wanted to impress but couldn't. You talk about her warm smile, her artistic talents, her secret ambitions, and her keen sensitivity to others.

You suddenly become for Peggy the parent who had time to listen, the teacher who talked about what was right about her instead of pointing out mistakes, the coach who put her in the game instead of keeping her on the sidelines, and, above all, the friend who was interested in *her* rather than what she looked like.

That attitude, in itself, can have a profound effect on others. Just look at them as capable, feeling, worthwhile human beings.

The story is told of the banker who often dropped a coin in the cup of the legless beggar who sat on the street outside the bank. But, unlike most people, the banker would always insist on getting one of the pencils the pauper had beside him. "You are a merchant," the banker would say, "and I always expect to receive good value from merchants I do business with."

One day the squat, hunched figure was not on the sidewalk. Time passed and the banker forgot about him, until he walked into a public building and there in the concessions stand sat the former vagrant. "I have always hoped you might come by someday," the storekeeper remarked. "You are largely responsible for me being here. You kept telling me I was a 'merchant.' I started thinking of myself that way, instead of a beggar receiving gifts. I started selling pencils—lots of them. You gave me self-respect, caused me to look at myself differently."

How do you see others? Do you view them critically, letting yourself be disturbed with the defects, failings, and traits they lack? Or do you see the goodness and wonders of people?

Do you perceive the beggar or the merchant in those about you?

Behind the masks that others wear from day to day is a little of the beggar or the Peggy. No matter how rich, famous, or successful they might appear, there is a hollowness that longs to be filled. Put a bit of you in that emptiness and the passing faces start pausing to look toward you. Those who have been far away are suddenly close. The world becomes a friendly place that meets your every need and wish before they are even expressed. People respond favorably; they do things for you.

What is being brought out here is the attitude you have toward people. Your success in dealing with them starts with the way you see them. Using a lot of tricky gimmicks, manipulative techniques, or psychological theories won't work. They'll see through those. This book has a lot of ideas of ways you can give people what they need. But they are only ideas. They are not guaranteed to work all the time. You'll have to fit them into your personality and relationships.

None of them will work, however, if they are used only to meet your selfish needs. Your interest in people must come from the heart. If you have that, if you genuinely care about others and want to help them become what they are capable of becoming, then you have a gift more beloved than the dearest jewel. Give it. Show your approval and appreciation! A bit of appreciation can be the most stirring force in a person's life!

THE IMPORTANCE OF APPRECIATION

A gifted executive, looking back on his career, realized how greatly his life had been influenced as a youth by a certain teacher. He traced her through the school, found that she was retired, and wrote her of his appreciation.

He received this reply:

"I can't tell you how much your note meant to me. I am in my eighties, living alone in a small room, cooking my own meals, lonely, and like the last leaf of fall lingering behind. You will be interested to know that I taught school for fifty years and yours is the first note of appreciation I have ever received. It came to me on a blue, cold morning, and it cheered me as nothing has in years."

It cheered me as nothing has in years! That sentence is a jolting revelation of the longing that people have for appreciation.

Although the nation has done a fair job of feeding the populace physically, there are millions going to bed every night starving emotionally for a few words or gestures of appreciation.

At the time the famed psychologist William James was working on his book, he was taken ill and confined to the hospital. A friend sent him an azalea plant and a note of appreciation. In expressing thanks for the plant, Dr. James said it brought to his attention an omission from his book.

He said he had neglected *the deepest quality of human nature— the craving to be appreciated!*

Giving appreciation makes the other person feel wanted, loved, needed. It helps one to like oneself.

Studies have shown that there is more job dissatisfaction caused by lack of appreciation than all other causes combined!

Surveys indicate that the greatest factor in marital tension is the inability of a partner to show appreciation.

B. C. Forbes wrote in *Forbes* magazine:

"No human being can be genuinely happy unless he or she stands well in the esteem of fellow mortals. He who would deal successfully with us must never forget that we possess and are possessed by this ego. A word of appreciation often can accomplish what nothing else could accomplish."

APPRECIATION STARTS WITH ACCEPTANCE

Actually, appreciation is only one leg of a three-legged pedestal that preserves every human relationship.

The three legs are the Triple A's that support any meaningful person-to-person association. They are Acceptance, Approval, and Appreciation.

Every heart cries out for acceptance. "Accept me! Although I am of a different age, sex, belief, race, job, or country than yours, accept me! I need to know that I am welcome to the human race. I must feel in my heart the oneness with, the belonging to, the life that I see about me. I don't know that unless you tell me in some way. A smile, a warm word, a kind act, anything at all to indicate that you accept me. For if you accept me, then I can accept myself, and we can go on from there and build something between us. But first I need to be accepted."

In a gloomy and depressed state, Eugene Field once wandered into a restaurant. A busy waiter hastened up and reeled off at high speed a long line of dishes on the menu. Field gazed up in melancholy and said, "Friend, I want none of those things. All I want is an orange and a few kind words."

A little attention, a few gracious words, is all it takes to indicate acceptance.

Ralph Waldo Emerson tells us, "Rings and jewels are not gifts, but apologies for gifts. The only gift is a portion of thyself."

Open up your world and let others come in! At every meeting with another, whether friend or stranger, you are at the threshold of a human encounter. You can open the door to your inner self just a crack and ask, "Who's there?" Or you can fling the door open and say, "Come in!" The first way you're holding people off; the other way you're accepting them. And that's what they want—*acceptance!* By giving them that, you have invited others to be your friend. Whether that be for the next few moments or a lifetime, they will then be seeking the second of the Triple A's—approval!

AFTER ACCEPTANCE COMES APPROVAL

I was backstage with a famous person who was about to address thousands in an auditorium.

"I'm petrified," he said. "My knees are shaking. My stomach feels like I'm on a roller coaster."

"Why are you frightened?" I asked.

"What if they don't like me? Maybe they won't approve of what I'm going to say!" he responded.

"What if they don't approve of me?" he was really saying. It's the nagging fear that persists in everyone's mind in all associations with others.

On Friday, May 20, 1977, a group of newspaper editors met with Jimmy Carter, who at that time had been President of the United States barely four months.

"It's a fairly pleasant life," President Carter said as he sat in the Cabinet Room of the White House, looking relaxed and good-humored.

One might wonder why he looked that way. It was the end of the week in which Congress had chewed on the limbs of his energy program, the Israeli public had dealt his Mideast peace hopes a blow, South Africa's prime minister had stonewalled Vice President Walter Mondale, and a U.S. general in Korea had grumbled that Carter's policies might be inviting war.

When asked if he minded the restraints that go with being President, Carter wistfully recalled how much worse the difficulties of campaigning had been.

"In the early stages of the campaign, I was really quite lonesome and isolated and often ignored and discouraged," Carter said. "At the beginning, I had to go looking for photographers."

What was he saying? At the beginning he had had to go looking for acceptance and approval. But when more than forty million voters indicated their approval of him, he could endure almost any controversy with ease and confidence.

That should give you some sort of a clue for dealing with people. Communicate acceptance and approval to your children, marriage partner, or working associates, and the relationship will stand stone solid against any strife or dispute. Give them your vote of approval. Let them know you accept them as worthwhile individuals. Stand behind them. Show keen interest in their thoughts and opinions, even if different from yours. Do these things, and you're ready to give them that which they desire most—appreciation.

SHOW YOUR APPRECIATION

The story is told of the woman who had worked hard raising a family with little appreciation from the family.

One evening she asked her husband, "I suppose, Peter, that if I should die you would spend a large amount for flowers for me, wouldn't you?"

"Of course I would, Martha. Why do you ask?"

"I was just thinking that the twenty-dollar wreaths would mean very little to me then. But just one little flower from time to time while I am living would mean so much to me."

Wasn't Martha really voicing the heartfelt hunger throbbing within the breast of all the people you see? "Just a little flower from time to time" gives people the basic hope and joy of their living.

Why wait until the hearts have stopped loving, the eyes are unseeing, and the ears are not listening?

Why do people hold back their expressions of appreciation? Maybe friction has worn down gratitude; hurt has dwarfed admiration. It could be that the scarcity of appreciation has diluted its flavor. Or perchance there's a less than noble little voice squeaking: "If you don't get it, don't give it!"

DON'T LET SELF-CONCERN HOLD YOU BACK

How about you? Are you generous with your appreciation for others? Or do you hang on to the illusion that all you are is what you have built by yourself?

You know, deep within you, that is not true. You are the child of all whom you have known. Each has woven in a bit of the color that makes the pattern of who you are. Search beyond the shallowness of false pride and, like the executive who wrote the schoolteacher, recognize the contributions others have made to your existence.

Look beyond your aggravations, irritations, justifications, and rationalizations. Put out of mind the many times others have pained you, upset you, trod over you. See instead those moments when, because of them, you rose to something you had never been before. You grew.

Cherish those who have touched your life and, in so doing, pressed you into being what you are today. They, in their stumbling, fumbling ways, may have caused you to cry or rebel or fret with anger. Their love and concern might have been disguised with impatience, criticism, restriction, and worry. But those are only indications that they cared. So gaze about you. Who can you find to appreciate?

START WITH THOSE AROUND YOU

How about your parents? Perhaps you have been hiding appreciation beneath the assumption that they know you care for them. Or you may have some repressed thoughts that you should have been given additional attention, restricted less, and praised more.

How about your children? Of course you love them, care for them, make sacrifices for them, feel an intense desire to mold them into worthy adults. But do you like them, enjoy them, show appreciation for them as human beings—just as they are?

And that man or woman with whom you're living? Do you restrain appreciation for all that person has done for you because you are suspicious that your criticisms and complaints will be forgotten? Do you suppose that if you show appreciation the consideration given you will dwindle?

You see, you are never loved quite the way you think you should be loved. It becomes difficult, therefore, to express appreciation for the love you have received. Your mind plays tricks on you about those who are closest to you. It tells you to withhold your appreciation because that will make the other person try harder, eventually bringing you the satisfaction you want.

But that is an attempt to use the rule backward, isn't it? That is saying, "Give me what I need, then I'll give you what you need." In rare instances that might work. One becomes so hungry for appreciation that untiring efforts are expended to receive approval or acceptance. But in the process, that individual may become bitter and resentful and develop a dwarfed self-concept. How much better for the person to grow freely and happily, stimulated by words and acts of appreciation.

BE THANKFUL FOR WHAT YOU HAVE

Think, for a time, of all that others have done for you—every sign of devotion, act of kindness, gesture of confidence, and extension of friendship. Have you shown your appreciation to the parent for simply being the parent, the employer for employing you, friends for being your friends, employees for spending precious days of their lives working for you, the mate's sacrifices and love, the customer's patronage, and the efforts of those who serve you? Pause long enough, every day, to show appreciation for the richness and fulfillment these people have brought into your life.

Make known your appreciation and you will discover endless rewards flowing to you. Humanity is attracted like bees to honey to those who extend acceptance, approval, and appreciation. Likewise, they are repelled by those who bury appreciation beneath their own self-centeredness. Surveys examining why customers stop doing business with department stores bear this out: one percent die, three percent move away, five percent change because of a friend's recommendation, nine percent leave for competitive reasons, fourteen percent are dissatisfied with the products, and sixty-eight percent stop coming back because of attitudes of indifference by some employee.

How do you express appreciation?

Do it in the way that's most comfortable for you. Many folks would be terribly uneasy tossing their arms around others and saying, "I love you." It doesn't have to be done that way to carry the message of regard and gratitude. Little gestures and casual words can add up to a heap of heartwarming. But try to be different, avoid the predictable. Appreciation means most when it is least expected.

So, with those thoughts in mind, just start flying! Open the floodgates and let esteem for others flavor your every word and act. Don't be too mindful of how it is done. Just share yourself like this, for these are the sights and sounds of appreciation:

Smile. Ask someone to lunch. Share yourself. Write a note. Hold a hand. Make someone's day a little better. Buy a gift. Say something nice about another. Do a favor. Lend a book. Phone a friend. Speak well of others. Send a card. Say "Thank you."

The list could go on and on. Try to add to it. For the rest of your life.

It is difficult to sort out the need for appreciation from the other needs people have. Actually, all the other suggestions in this book are symbols of appreciation. Praise, listening, understanding, making others feel important—all are ways of projecting your respect and admiration for those about you.

So don't try to separate humans into compartments or this book into segments. Search behind the sentences for the feelings involved. Allow those emotions to become your emotions. Then go out and share them with everyone you meet.

That's appreciation.

It has something to do with love, too, doesn't it?

4

What Motivates People

"I worked for that company six years ago. Here, just a minute, let me show you something."

The businessman opened his desk drawer and pulled out a white sheet of paper with mimeographed printing on it.

Handing me the paper, he said, "I was their top salesman out of 150 one month."

Sure enough, there was his name heading the list of the company's first ten sales people for one month seven years ago.

It was a casual incident that took place in the man's office while discussing the management policies of a certain company. Casual, that is, unless you're looking past the modest smile and offhanded air in which the episode was brought up. For there, pounding beneath the surface, was the pulse of one person's existence.

Let's pull it out, look backstage and see what really happened. Seven years ago he was one of 150, lost in a shuffle of bodies. Someone else was getting the credit, carrying away the trophies, receiving the attention that he longed for.

Then in one burst, for thirty days, he surged forward. Two weeks into that golden month he probably realized that he had a chance, for once in his life, to win a race, to be somebody. During those final two weeks he most likely drove himself desperately to stay ahead of the rest, working day and night for every dollar's worth of business.

The final day came, the finish line was crossed, and he was the one who broke the tape! He was the star. He couldn't wait to tell his wife.

"I did it. I was number one," he said that evening, trying to hide the gleam of pride. "Let's go out and celebrate."

"I think that's wonderful," she glowed, throwing her arms around him. "I'm so proud of you."

The next day at the office he was the halfback who had raced for the winning touchdown on the team he had never been able to make before. He was David after whipping Goliath, the movie idol who had come back home, the small town lad who had won the nomination for president.

The mimeographed sheet came out naming him the leader. It might as well have been the local newspaper with his name in the headlines! The loser, the guy who had been running with the pack all these years, had broken out and was declared the winner. At last, a champion!

It all lasted for such a precious few hours. Then another month and another leader. The only fragment of those glorious days was a piece of paper. But he clung to that. It was beside him as he went into his own little business. There was the blazing headline, the remembrance of those hours of fame, a mimeographed sheet in his top desk drawer, still there seven years later.

THE COMMON THRUST IN PEOPLE'S LIVES

Unreal, you say? Not at all. It's about as real as monthly payments, apple pie, the national anthem, tennis shoes, Christmas trees, and owning a car.

The whole incident is part of the warp and woof of the average individual's existence. The only mistake would be to underestimate the significance of those seemingly insignificant episodes of recognition in people's lives.

That episode said what most of those around you are saying. They thirst for recognition, for being somebody important. In the last chapter we dealt with the craving for acceptance and appreciation. Is that enough? No. People's needs go beyond that. They want to stand out, be noticed, made to feel important. Recognition, a few ribbons tagged on their chests, does that for them.

The efforts to get special attention start at an early age. "Come here, Mommy. Look at the sand castle I made," cries the child at the beach.

The tiny face peeking around the corner of the newspaper, a tug on the pants leg, the beaming smile of pride that goes with the freshly picked bouquet of dandelions are all simple requests saying, "Notice me!"

A substantial part of children's behavior that parents might call "naughtiness" is only the outcropping of the wish for recognition. It doesn't end when school starts. The results of giving recognition to children in the classroom are so overwhelmingly positive that it is accepted as the significant stimulant to learning.

Gold stars, being the classroom messenger to the principal's office, special privileges, a name on a blackboard, a compliment, and all the many other ways of recognizing children, making them feel important, are part of the spawning process in which those little humans flourish.

Denying attention to children is rejection. That creates antagonism, anti-social attitudes, all sorts of behavior problems. Nothing very complicated about it. Rejection is painful. Recognition pleases, heals.

It's a characteristic that never changes much in the life cycle.

Walk through a nursing home, the kind of place where there are those living their last days under one roof. Pause long enough before each one to smile, nod, or speak a kind word. Faces will break into joy, hands will reach out to be touched, words will pour out, "Don't go. Stay and talk with me. Give me your attention! Notice me!"

RECOGNITION CAN INFLUENCE LIVES

You are never quite sure of the intensity of the need for attention in others. All you know is that it exists and is probably more desperately needed than you realize. This letter, written to Ann Landers,* the daily newspaper confidante, is a solemn reminder of that:

Dear Ann: Last December a pal of mine killed himself. Another friend attempted suicide three times in the past 14 months. I tried to take my own life a few years ago.

We all had promising futures and financial security, but we lacked one thing—the ability to relate to others. I stopped wanting to kill myself when I realized my death would make a difference. That somebody really cared.

If people want to help, they can. Here are a few things everyone can do: Smile more—even to people you don't know. Touch people. Look them in the eye. Let them know you are aware they exist. Be concerned about those you work with. Listen when they speak to you. Spend an extra minute. If someone has a problem, just listening means more than you'll ever know.

To those who are in depression, say this: "Everybody has highs and lows. Nobody is on top of the world all the time. You'll crawl back up again if you give yourself a chance. Tomorrow will be better."

You could save a life without realizing it by letting a depressed person know somebody cares. I care.—Age 27

On the other hand, that same incessant itching to be noticed by others can drive an individual to almost impossible accomplishments.

David Kunst left a surveying job and his wife and three children in Waseca, Minnesota, to do what no individual had

---

*Ann Landers, Field Newspaper Syndicate.

previously accomplished. He and his brother, John, set out to circle the globe on foot.

John Kunst died two years later, when the brothers were ambushed by Afghanistan bandits. David, shot in the chest, survived. He resumed the world walk.

The trek was completed four and a half years after it started. Why would a man slice out a chunk of his life to spend in such a desolate ordeal?

The answer might be found in these words of his: "I should have been a movie star or something. I like fame. I mean, I've got to admit it, I just enjoy having my name in the paper."

If human beings will go to such extremes to be noticed, imagine what they will do for you if you can satisfy, even for a few moments, that ever-present appetite for recognition!

Here are some ways to do that.

Giving Praise

Cleve Backster, a lie detection expert, acting on impulse after working late in his office in 1966, wired a polygraph machine to the leaf of a *Dracaena massangeana* to gauge any response to water poured on the house plant's roots.

The polygraph showed a response. Intrigued, Backster dunked one of the plant's leaves into his cup of hot coffee. No reaction. So he conceived a worse threat. He decided to burn the electrode-attached leaf.

As soon as he pictured the burning leaf in his mind, there was a dramatic change—a long upward sweep of the recording pen on the graph. Since then Backster and others have conducted extensive studies linking plant life to the emotions and attitudes of humans. The results prove conclusively that plants reflect what is shown them. When they are admired and praised, they thrive and fill the air with their lovely life. But when shunned and condemned they become stunted and sickly.

If human beings have this effect on plants, think how much more powerful is the effect they have on each other!

Phillips Brooks said it this way: "To say, 'well done' to any bit of good work is to take hold of the powers which have made the effort and strengthen them beyond our knowledge!"

"We are all excited by the love of praise," wrote Cicero.

Praise spurs people to achieve, gives them inner confidence, and makes them grow.

A psychologist once told me, "There is no mystery to raising children. Just praise them. When they eat right, praise them. When they draw a picture, praise them. When they learn to ride a bike, praise them."

It has been said that one's life is spent avoiding punishment or working for rewards. Praise is a reward people work for. It shapes and stimulates behavior.

Students in a university experiment were divided into three groups. The first group was given a great deal of encouragement and praise. The second group was virtually ignored. The third group was given nothing but criticism. The ignored group progressed the least, the criticized group made some progress, but the praised group achieved outstanding results!

I have had my students in personality and human relations classes practice giving compliments. Each one stands in front of the class and gives some member a specific compliment.

Besides having it make everyone feel good, it has revealed a peculiarity of human nature. It was expressed by one student after being complimented about his smile by a friend, "I have known that person for fifteen years and that is the first time he has ever mentioned that he even noticed that I smiled!"

Why is this? Why do people withhold their praise?

I was once conducting a workshop for a number of married couples. I asked each individual to write down fifteen good things about the spouse. In fact, I offered a little prize for the first one to complete the project.

Soon, one person stood up with the finished list.

The sad aspect of the whole episode was that some had not made the first mark on the paper yet. What an empty, ungratified relationship! Imagine people living together who cannot or will not write down a single good thing about the other!

When I got home that evening I immediately sat down and wrote a list of sixty-seven good things about my wife. By doing that I discovered it was a way to gain recognition and immortality as an author. She might throw away the books, articles, and unfinished manuscripts I've written. But she will never part with that list!

Try it! Do the same for members of your family. Bring them together. Have them compile a list of at least fifteen good things about each other. Or, better yet, see who can develop the longest list. Then take the idea to the job. Get people to do it who work together. You'll find it's a wonderful activity for a church gathering or Sunday school class.

You can guarantee the individuals writing the lists that they have achieved a status that even the most prominent writers never achieve. Their work will never be thrown away.

Although it is looked upon as an enjoyable little exercise, those receiving the lists of fifteen good things about themselves will save those pieces of paper as long as they live!

Those words of praise strike deeply. They satisfy, nourish, soothe, and stir up warm feelings.

How many such flowers go ungiven? How many compliments go unsaid? How many people do you admire for certain qualities or accomplishments but have never bothered saying so?

Why not say it?

Why not practice praising?

Why not start looking for ways to compliment others? When you do, consider these thoughts:

Be sincere. Don't give false flattery. But being sincere is just a matter of looking for the good in others. You'll find it if you're sincerely looking!

Be specific. Don't just say a person is "nice" or "good." Pick out specific things to praise.

Praise what a person does instead of the person. It's more

genuine. It means more that way. Besides, it avoids making the other person feel embarrassed.

But most important—SAY IT! Get over being shy about giving praise. Don't hold it back. It can be so tremendously cherished by others! Give it whenever you can.

Giving Status

In 1917, Russia took all status away from its officers. Officers swabbed their own quarters, ate with the rank and file, and stood in line with the orderlies. They received no special privileges, salutes, or titles. Overnight, the organization sank into the most awful mess of an army history has ever known.

The officers were completely demoralized. They were worthless as soldiers, to say nothing of how they fulfilled their responsibilities as officers.

As soon as it became obvious what had happened, Russia restored full status to its officers.

In its monstrous blunder, Russia had overlooked one glaring, compelling thrust of human behavior. Russia found that to get things done in an organized society you must give people prestige! They learned their lesson well. Today in Russia medals, trophies, and titles are used generously to give distinction to all segments of their society.

People will often work harder for a title, special privilege, or plaque than they will for financial reward.

Athletes will devote thousands of grueling hours to training, spurred by the hope of winning a trophy or becoming a champion.

Status need not be limited to athletics or organizations. Giving prominence and position to another can be done in a variety of ways.

Any attention that you give to people makes them feel noticed, recognized, important.

Pause long enough with the child and ask, "What are you making?"

To the person checking out your groceries you might say, "Your fingers must get strong working them like that every day. You should play the piano or guitar!"

As you go to work Monday morning, greet the first person you see with, "Hi! Did you have a nice weekend?"

The purpose is to get in the habit of being friendly to people. Show interest. Make comments. Ask sincere questions. Treat people with respect and dignity, as if they counted for something. Here's another way to do that.

Being Courteous

When Marshal Foch was in this country on a mission during World War I, he was cornered by a nervy cynic who launched into a tirade against French politeness.

"There is nothing in it but wind," he sneered.

'There is nothing in a tire but wind," politely replied the Marshal, "but it makes riding in a car quite smooth and pleasant."

John Wanamaker, the master merchant, once said, "Courtesy is the one coin we can never have too much of, nor ever be stingy with." Following that principle brought him wealth and fame.

"The whole of heraldry and chivalry," wrote Emerson, "is in courtesy!"

I was talking to a friend who had escorted a famous author and lecturer visiting the city. My friend spent several hours with the celebrity, meeting him at the airport and providing him with transportation in the city.

"What impressed you most about him?" I asked.

"When he opened the door for me and gently pushed me through first," responded my friend. "It was typical of his fine manners."

There is no characteristic of human nature that is as exchangeable as courtesy. You give it—it is returned to you—and the other person feels good. Courtesy strokes the other person into feeling important. In contrast, there is no more brutal attack on a person's ego than discourtesy. To treat a person with disregard and discourtesy is to kindle their belligerence and hostility.

If you're going to convince or persuade a person to do anything, the first ten seconds of your association is probably the most important. People form impressions quickly. There is nothing more difficult for you to overcome than a bad first impression. Samuel Goldwyn said, "The first impressions you make are usually the most important. Even though it may be years later, people will usually remember whether you were courteous or rude."

Being courteous will start your association with others on a warm, friendly basis. It is "good first impression insurance!"

But don't limit your good manners to strangers! Exercise politeness and gentility with those closest to you. Be liberal with "Thank you" and "Please."

Never take for granted those favors and chores that others are always doing for you. If you do, your relationships will slide into dullness and complacency. Freshen them with politeness, respect, appreciation.

Apologizing

It was an early morning breakfast flight from Minneapolis to St. Louis. The plane departed fifteen minutes late, the coffee was sloshed around on the tray by mild turbulence, and then there was a fifteen-minute wait to get into the St. Louis airport. Passengers were getting a little grumpy.

But then the captain came on the intercom. "I want to apologize for the choppy ride this morning. We've been looking around for a little smooth air at some altitude, but it's hard to find. Sorry. But I hope you've enjoyed your breakfast. Thank you for flying with us."

Shortly after that we were on the ground and the stewardess

announced, "We want to apologize for the air traffic delay coming in. I hope it hasn't inconvenienced any of you too greatly and that you have a nice day in St. Louis."

About then I wanted to say, "Aw, heck, it wasn't your fault the air was bumpy and the plane was late. You don't have to apologize." They didn't have to, but they did. And I felt brighter, as if the unpleasantries had been bagged and placed aside.

That's the way a casual apology affects people. It's a way of lifting a little load off the mind of another and shoving it aside so that no ill feeling exists.

Saying you're sorry or apologizing is no big thing. It's an emotional pacifier, soothing to the jagged corners of someone's feelings.

A few words of regret is a way of saying you care, a show of sensitivity to the ragged edges of another's emotion. What difference does it make whose fault it was? Get it behind you with a little verbal peace offering. You'll make the other person feel better.

People need that once in a while. The world keeps putting pebbles in one's shoes. Walking along becomes more uncomfortable. It's nice to have someone come along and take a few out.

"I'm sorry. You shouldn't have to put up with that."

"I apologize. You were treated unfairly."

"I don't blame you if you're upset. I regret that happened."

Someone cares! Another understands! The clouds have parted and the day shines!

Apologies, symbols of sympathy, seem to be verbal trifles, throwaway words that some don't consider of enough significance to bother saying. But life is a mass of specks and drops, tiny happenings that are pluses or minuses. Anything, no matter how small, that you can contribute of a plus nature to those about you makes you a special quantity in their lives.

Using Names

People are like balloons—every time their names are heard or seen, it's just like a shot of air. It makes them swell up!

Remember Achilles, the Greek warrior? He had only one mortal weakness—his heel! His heel was pierced by an arrow and it killed him.

Every mortal has an "Achilles heel." It's their name!

People will work, will strive, will sacrifice, will give effort and money, will pull themselves to new heights just to see or hear their own names. Learn to use others' names successfully and you will build a new power into your personality.

Jim Farley, former Postmaster General and a political genius, was said to have a memory for over fifty thousand first names and faces. He became famous for his ability to call people by their first names. They loved it and made him a powerful figure in American government.

I know a talented young executive who quickly rose to the presidency of his company. He produced spectacular records in company growth.

As a result, he was offered a remarkable position by a much larger rival company. The offer meant thousands of dollars more to him each year besides stock options and other benefits.

When he told the directors of his present company he was going to resign, one of the directors came up with a remarkable idea. They couldn't begin to match the rival offer, but they did tell my friend they would use his name in the company name.

He withdrew his resignation. Chances are that he will stay a lifetime with the same company because it bears his name.

If you want people to do things for you, use their names.

A program chairman for a large community event told me this incident.

He wanted to get members for his committee, so he phoned fifteen people. All of them were "just too busy" to serve. "I had to do something," he told me, "to get people to volunteer to do some work. So I decided to print their names on the program."

"When I called the next ten people, I told them we wanted to print their names on the program. Then I asked if they would be willing to serve on our committee so that we could do this. All ten accepted!"

Use people's names! It's a beautiful sound to them, like dropping jewels into the palms of their hands. It's the one tool you can use over and over and over and people never tire of it. It weakens resistance, dilutes antagonism, and softens opposing views.

How to Remember Names

Most people know how important remembering names can be, but they say, "I have a poor memory. I just can't remember names."

They are wrong. Everyone has a good memory. They just don't know how to use it. Here are some simple rules for using your memory to remember names.

Start saying, "I Have the World's Best Memory for Names!" Stop telling yourself you can't remember names. Stop being afraid you'll forget. Stop being fearful you'll call someone by a wrong name. As long as you feed into your mind doubt, hesitation, and fear about names, that's the kind of results you'll get.

Want to Remember Names? If someone gave you one hundred dollars for every person's name you could remember, how much difficulty would you have? You would probably be out looking for every stranger you could meet just so that you could remember his name and collect the money!

You only remember those things you want to remember. Perhaps no one will pay you one hundred dollars for each name, but they will repay you many times in efforts and friendliness if you learn to remember their names.

Get the Name Right. Such questions as these are music to the other person's ears:

"Would you pronounce your name again, please?"

"How do you spell your name?"

"Do I pronounce your name right?"

Remember, the other person's name sounds wonderful! Having you talk about it is great! Don't be embarrassed by asking if you have it right.

Say the Name Three Times Immediately.   Tests have shown you remember or forget something within the first hour of being exposed to it. Use the name at least three times after hearing it so that you can impress it into your memory. Then reinforce it by associating it with as many pictures as possible. Where you met the person, things the name reminded you of, and "picturing" the name in your mind are useful in remembering names.

Write It Down.   At the end of the day write down the names of new people you've met. If you have a diary, day book, or calendar of your schedule, jot names in one of these. Keep a file of the organizations to which you belong. Write the names of people as you meet them in each of the files. Before you attend a function of a group, quickly review the names. Soon, of course, the person will become familiar enough so that the name will be easily recalled.

Most individuals I know whose work requires that they meet a lot of new people have a similar system. The point is that they realize the significance of people's names. They know it's worth a little effort to remember the one or two words that make another feel a little special.

Remembering

"You probably don't recall the lunch we had fifteen years ago, but you asked me then if I was happy; if I was doing what I really wanted to do. That lunch started my thoughts in a direction that changed my life."

And those words made my activities that afternoon a shade more buoyant. Someone remembered! Imagine! I said something fifteen years ago that had been hung on to by another person.

That's the kind of remembering that means the most. Birthdays, anniversaries, and holidays are all fitting times to send cards to friends. It's always pleasing to get mail and know someone is thinking about you.

But what really causes warm vibrations is when people let you know that you have done something unexpected to put grooves in their memories.

"The last time we met you were building a ship in a bottle. How is it coming?"

"Did you finish that sweater you were knitting?"

"How does your daughter like college?"

"It was your idea that we send thank-you letters to customers. It was eight years ago you thought of that."

"I'll never forget that putt you sank on the 15th at Hilldale four years ago."

"Did you ever think more of taking that evening course? A year ago you mentioned it."

"I still think about that evening we ate at the Brookshire. You wore that beige dress I like so much."

Tones of remembering! Unlooked-for pieces of the past that you agreeably hear are on the shelf of someone's mind! How nice that the person mentioned it!

There are dozens of other ways to recognize people, to put them on a pedestal and stroke the egos that the world so customarily ignores. Whether you use the ideas here or ones of your own making is of little consequence. It is, however, of vital significance that you emphasize the uniqueness and wonder of every human being you meet. You will never fully comprehend the impact you can have on others' lives by building them up by special recognition.

Give thoughtful attention to every person's matchless qualities, not just certain people with whom you want to ingratiate yourself.

All people are beautiful and special. Practice making them feel that way.

The waitress who serves you a cup of coffee, the elevator

operator, the clerk, the boss, the next-door neighbor, the stranger you pass on the street, the man who comes to pick up your garbage, the janitor who cares for your office building, the child who delivers your paper, the teacher, the preacher, the barber, the mail carrier—the whole panorama of people who enter your life for only brief moments—all are worth the thoughtful effort it takes to make them feel important!

Incidentally, be prepared to feel pretty good about yourself. Because what you give to others is going to be given back to you!

5

Removing Conflict and Irritation from Relationships

It was a cold winter morning. The shopping center parking lot was ridged with piles of fresh snow heaped high by the wind and plows. I parked my car and headed for the sidewalk, the only exit that had been freed from the drifts of snow.

But there was a car left directly in front of the shoveled pathway! I had to trudge around the vehicle, wading into snow up to my knees, to get onto the walk.

"How thoughtless can people be!"

The words ran through my mind along with a few less printable ones. Arriving at one of the entry doors of the shopping center, I stamped my feet to shake the snow off my trousers and turned to bore a few angered glares in the side of the car.

There, struggling along the walk, was a lady with crutches extending from both arms, her legs encased in braces. Slowly, ever so slowly, she inched her way along the slippery pathway, got to the car blocking the walk, tussled herself into the front seat, and drove away.

I stood for a moment, shamed that I had felt the way I had. My anger and irritation, of course, were whisked away like the snow I had brushed from my legs only moments before.

In seconds I had changed. But what had changed me? The situation was the same. The car was still barricading the sidewalk; the stacks of snow were there to be waded through. The only variation was my attitude toward the situation.

I saw the woman and her plight. Suddenly I *understood!*

And with my changed attitude of understanding, annoyance and judgment melted away.

There you have it! The absolutely indispensable ingredient to getting along with others is understanding! Human associations go astray where there is no understanding. Differences, displeasures, wrath, frustration, conflict, and separation start where understanding stops.

If you would be a giant in getting things done with people, you must first acquire understanding.

I could have told myself it was excusable that I was provoked about the car obstructing the pathway. OK. Maybe. But if I accepted that, how many of my other negative attitudes toward those around me would I try to justify?

It's typical of people to sit in judgment of others day in and day out. If they don't act the way we think they should, then we get upset, even though it is often only to a slight degree. Still, that's enough to add a little tension or strain to the encounter.

During seminars on human relations that I have conducted, I have asked this question: "Do any of you feel that you don't get along with others?" Very seldom will someone raise a hand.

Then I ask them to write down their three greatest pet peeves. One sampling of a thousand of these responses was indicative of the usual results: 998 of their biggest gripes in life *were caused by other people!*

What, then, are people truly saying by their answers to these two questions? Just this: "I feel I get along with you fine and dandy until you do something I don't like. Then I stop getting along with you, inside. I become irritated, aggravated, frustrated."

And that's no way to feel if one is going to establish a pleasant association with another, to say nothing of getting that other person to act in a certain way or do something productive. The only emotional chemistry that will dissolve those smoldering feelings is understanding.

That is no new revelation. In Proverbs 14:29 it is revealed: "He that is slow of wrath is of great understanding!"

And Solomon, in all of his wisdom, asked for only one thing: "Give therefore thy servant an understanding heart to judge people!"

Plato and Aristotle both recognized and sought understanding. Its importance is proclaimed in Proverbs 3:13:

> Happy is the man that findeth wisdom, and the man that getteth understanding.
> For the merchandise of it is better than the merchandise of silver, and the gain thereof than fine gold.
> She is more precious than rubies: and all the things thou canst desire are not to be compared to her.
> Length of days is in her right hand: and in her left hand riches and honour.
> Her ways are ways of pleasantness, and all her paths are peace.
> She is a tree of life to them that lay hold upon her: and happy is everyone that retaineth her.
> The Lord by wisdom hath founded the earth; by understanding he established the heavens.

CHECK YOUR ABILITY TO UNDERSTAND

How is your understanding? To get a handle on the importance of this ability in dealing with others, put yourself into these situations.

You are driving a new car along a road. There is a small boy standing beside the road waving his arm. As you pass him, he throws something at your car. A crunching thud resounds on the side of your car! You realize he has hit it with a rock.

You jam on your brakes, climb out of the car, and start back toward the boy. With each step you become more upset. You think of the action you will take. The boy should be taken to his parents with the demand that they pay for the damage.

By the time you reach the boy, your blood pressure has reached the boiling point.

There he stands, tearful and frightened. He looks up and says, "I was sorry to do that, but it was the only way I knew to stop your car."

Then he points to a figure in the deep grass and adds, "My little brother has been hurt real bad. Will you help him?"

Now what happens to your anger and temper? It has vanished like an icicle in a flame! Why? Because you now understand why this boy did this to you! In your judgment of him he was acquitted; with his acquittal went your exasperation and anger.

THE CHALLENGE OF UNDERSTANDING

Let's try another. Your sister is married to a successful attorney. In recent months his attitude toward her has changed. He has become suspicious, domineering, and even restrictive of her actions.

At family gatherings he follows her when she leaves the room. He will not let her leave their home alone. She has complained that he will not even allow her to go to the store alone to shop.

You become so resentful of the way he is treating your sister that you decide to discuss it with other members of your family. You all agree that something should be done.

And then you receive a telephone call from a psychologist. He wants you to come to his office. When you get there, he asks you to reveal any memories you have about your sister's early childhood. He explains that she has become a kleptomaniac; she has acquired an uncontrollable impulse to steal. He points out, also, the burden your brother-in-law is bearing in order that her sickness be veiled from the community.

Has your feeling about him changed now? Are you still hateful and resentful? Probably not, because now you understand his behavior.

UNDERSTANDING IN BUSINESS

You are an insurance salesperson. You and your spouse have a bridge date for Thursday evening. On Thursday morning you are talking with a prospect; he agrees to bring his wife to your office to discuss a policy. Thursday evening is the only possible time that he can meet with you.

Reluctantly you call home. You ask that the bridge date be cancelled. Of course, there is disappointment at the other end of the line.

You stay at the office that evening instead of going home for dinner. You run out for a sandwich and a cup of coffee; it's a rainy, chilly evening. You feel just a bit sorry for yourself that you have to be working instead of relaxing in the warm surroundings of a home and friends.

You wait in the office for the prospect. The time of the appointment passes—no prospect. A half hour passes. Still no prospect. After an hour you call the prospect's home. No answer. After an hour and a half, you lock the office and go home. You are fuming. "At least," you tell yourself, "they could have had the decency to call."

Your evening is spoiled. Still upset and annoyed, you go to bed. You feel this is one prospect you are entitled to "tell off."

At nine o'clock the next morning you are at your desk. The telephone rings. It is the prospect.

"I want to apologize," he explains, "for not being at your office last night. On the way there we had a rather bad accident. The streets were slippery and another car collided with ours. I'm calling from the hospital where we have been since last night. I would have called you last night, but we were pretty upset."

Are you still "mad" at them? Do you still think they are thoughtless, irresponsible, and should be "told off"? No, of course not. Now it is you who feels half guilty because the accident happened on the way to meet you.

Now you understand!

EMPLOYEES NEED TO BE UNDERSTOOD

Assume that you are an office manager. One of the secretaries habitually leaves five minutes earlier than she is supposed to. At ten minutes to five she starts clearing her desk; at five minutes to five she darts out the front door.

One of your "pet peeves" is a clock watcher. If this secretary did not do such an excellent job, you would have spoken to her before about this habit of leaving five minutes early. However, your resentment mounts to a point that finally compels you to speak your mind.

You call her into your office, preparing to reprimand her. You begin by revealing to her that her actions have not gone unnoticed. You ask her if she has any explanation.

"Yes, I believe I have," she replies. "You see, I am a widow and the sole support of three small children. A woman cares for my children during the day, but she must leave at 5:45. If I get the 5:00 bus I get home at 5:45. If I do not, the next bus does not leave until 5:45 and gets me home at 6:30. I cannot leave my three small children unattended for that 45 minutes. I did not want to mention this because I was afraid that I would have to leave my job."

Are you still incensed? Still irritated? Not if you are like the office manager who actually had this experience. Because after the explanation he understood. He promptly made special arrangements with the company for her to leave five minutes early and make up the time on special occasions.

These are examples of situations involving other people that can result in nettled, annoyed feelings.

In your daily life you are exposed to a whole parade of instances similar to these that may cause that quick spurt of grinding emotion named "irritation." At work you become irritated with the person who interrupts you, talks too much, loafs a bit, is inconsiderate. On the road the other driver is going too fast or too slow, is too close behind or cuts ahead of you. Life in a family may produce a whole batch of continuous conflicts and irritations.

If you allow yourself to react spontaneously to this array of episodes you will probably find life to be a steady stream of emotional bumps and bruises. Besides making you miserable, your negative feelings can cause you to be downright sick.

So it's wise to realize that you cannot go through life controlling situations, circumstances, and people. But you can control your attitudes toward them. And with an attitude of understanding you are removing a large measure of your displeasure and, at the same time, giving people exactly what they need and crave. They are begging for it. Every beat of their hearts is pleading, "Please understand me!"

YOU CAN FILL A DEEP HUMAN NEED

People hunger and strive to be understood by others. This longing is bred from the enigma that one does not understand oneself. Socrates' immortal words, "Know thyself," implied a search—not a destination.

This is one thing that nearly all inmates in prisons have in common. They say, "I don't know why I did what I did. It wasn't my fault. I'm not to blame. Please, understand this—and me!"

A minister told me of an unruly young lad who came to see him one day. He had been in all kinds of trouble and scrapes. His first words were, "I must find someone who understands me."

One day I was explaining these concepts of understanding to a friend of mine, Dr. Jack Berg, a psychologist. Dr. Berg said, "You know—you're right. The human mind reaches for understanding like a flower for the sun!"

So there it is—the human need for understanding. What more powerful talent could you possess to get along with others than the ability to communicate and give others your gift of understanding?

Your husband or wife is saying, "I know I've been grumpy and spoken sharply to you, but before you turn me off and things get icy cold for the next couple of days, understand me. I haven't been feeling too good. I've been worried about the monthly payments; it seems like there's so much to do; and the kids get on my nerves. My back hurts and my head aches. Please, before you become exasperated with me and ignore me, understand me!"

How many homes have been broken because this need for understanding is not satisfied? You see men and women leaving love and respect in a vague, compelling search for understanding. The old story, "I'm not understood at home," has, perhaps, deeper implications than we realize.

And the employee is saying, "I know that I goof off sometimes, and I don't always put out like I should. Maybe I pop off when I shouldn't and it's true I did some griping in the lunchroom. But before you fire me or decide I'm not much good around here, understand me. Know that I've got problems at home. And I get tired of just standing and putting papers in files all day long. Please, understand me!"

The child is no different. "I'm flunking in that subject. But before you decide what you're going to do to me, Mom and Dad, understand me. Seems like I try but I just hate that course. And the teacher picks on me. The other day I had to go up in front of the class and I felt like a dummy. I know you're probably going to ground me for a week, but, please, just this once, understand me."

The prospect is telling the salesperson, "Just a minute, now. You're telling me all the reasons I should buy that product, and I know you've got a bag of tricks you've picked up along the way to get me to open my pocketbook. But how do you know I need what you're selling? You don't understand me."

In fact, as a result of an extensive survey in which buyers were asked what they disliked most about dealing with salespeople, this response outnumbered all others three to one: "The sales person didn't seem to really understand my problem!"

Maybe the salespeople felt differently. They might have been fired with conviction that their products were just what the prospects needed. But they failed to communicate understanding. And that's essential in any relationship. Understanding must be communicated. It cannot be taken for granted. It has to be expressed, verbally or nonverbally, in some way. Just the words themselves can be a balm to a troubled mind.

For example: You've had a busy, fretful day. You're worn out and anxious to settle down for the evening. You drive the car into the driveway and there's a tricycle sitting right in the middle of it. You get out of the car and shove the trike to one side, muttering, "I've told that kid a dozen times to keep the tricycle out of the driveway."

You park your car and tramp into the house, slamming the door behind you. Now what do you want to hear? "How come you're so crabby tonight?"

Wouldn't it be better to hear, "Well, you've had a rough day, haven't you? I understand how you feel."

That's about as simple a way to communicate understanding as there is. "I understand how you feel!" Remember that. Use it. Even with children. When those little eyes start flickering about apprehensively in the cabin of an airplane before take-off and words peep out, "I'm scared," don't start lecturing, "There's no need for you to feel that way. I'm right here and you're perfectly safe."

Instead, reach out, put that tiny hand in yours, lean over, and whisper, "I understand how you feel."

You'll get a sensitivity for when those words fit and when they don't. For there are times when people won't believe you can comprehend the hurt or pain or problem they are enduring.

"Don't tell me you know how I feel," they are thinking. "How do you know? You've never been me. You've never gone through what I'm going through. Have you ever been in deep water and can't swim? Ever been dumped by someone you love? I've got a bigger problem than you've handled before. You can't understand my position. You can't imagine the anguish, torment, pain, and worry I'm going through."

Maybe so. But you can communicate your understanding by acknowledging the other person's right to feel the way he or she does.

"You have a right to feel the way you do."

"I've never experienced that, but I think if I were in your place I'd feel the same way you do."

"I'll admit I don't know much about your problem. But if you'd like to tell me about it, I'll try to understand and help you any way I can."

KEEP YOURSELF IN CONTROL

Work your way along on this. If you sincerely want to express understanding, you will find ways to do it. I'll tell you what not to do. Whatever comes out of your mouth, don't let it be: "You shouldn't feel that way." Or, "How come you feel like that?" (with a quizzical expression). Or, "There is no reason for you to feel the way you do." If your logic is urging you to say something like that, stick your fist in your mouth. In your desire to be helpful it's so easy for those words to blunder out.

Your teenager comes in after school, gloomy and dejected. "I found out there's a big thing going on next Saturday and I wasn't asked. No one likes me. I don't have any friends at all."

So you come back with, "You shouldn't feel that way. You know you've got a lot of nice friends. And you always have your home."

Now you've blown it! It would have been better to say nothing.

Or the purchasing agent for one of your company's accounts calls, and daggers of fire start spurting out of the phone receiver. "I don't see how you people could have messed up that order so badly. This is the third time I've called, and you still haven't done anything about it."

Your first impulse is to put the person down with, "You have no reason to feel like that. The original mistake was made in your purchasing department and when we found out about it we took care of it immediately. If you'll check your other plant, where you asked us to send the order, you'll find it was received by your loading dock two days ago."

You might be right. But you're handling it wrong if you want the person to be on your side. You're not expressing understanding for the way the person feels.

Or you're confronted with, "I've got to get out of this house. Things are always in a mess. The kids get to me. It seems like I'm on a treadmill. I'm not doing anything worthwhile."

You might feel like saying, "How come you feel like that? You have three lovely children, a beautiful home, and every convenience there is. There are a lot of people who would be plenty thankful for everything you've got."

But don't say it! Not if you want to maintain a happy relationship. To do that, you must somehow communicate understanding; the other person has a right to those feelings. He or she wants to know that from you!

And, remember: To the degree you give others what they need they will give you what you need.

If you don't have understanding, forget about getting along with others, communicating with your children, forging ahead on a job, or developing deep, rich relationships with people around you.

It's a way of thinking you have to keep working at. Sometimes it will be difficult. And at times you will forget. But keep at it. The reactions you will start getting will be encouraging.

There are no surefire formulas for achieving understanding. If there were, we would have no wars, divorces, family splits, strikes, or crimes of violence. But there are some ideas and suggestions that, if people would follow them, would at least point them in the direction of being more understanding. The next chapter will explain those thoughts.

6

Putting Tolerance and Understanding into Your Life

How do you acquire understanding?

I don't believe you ever do, really.

Understanding, to me, is more of an attitude than an ability. An individual can never have a complete knowledge or comprehension of the experiences and conditioning that make another person what he or she is. I don't even understand myself and why I act the way I do sometimes. How can I possibly understand you?

Perhaps that, in itself, explains understanding. It's the realization that we are both human beings. We carry on in unexplainable ways. We behave according to emotion rather than logic. And there's nothing dumber than our emotions. Why do we laugh? Why do we cry? What puts us in a good mood one day and a bad mood the next? Why should we get angry with someone we love? Why do we like one person more than another? Why do we do some of the silly, goofy, often regrettable things we do and then ask ourselves, "What makes me act this way?"

The answers to those questions have something to do with emotions, opinions, attitudes, experiences, habits, and a lot of little episodes that may have been long forgotten. Maybe understanding is a realization of all of that. It might be knowing that however irrational another person seems to be there are reasons for that behavior and that if you or I lived with those same reasons we probably would be somewhat the same way.

Getting one's mind to roll on tracks like that instead of reacting negatively to people and situations will go a long way toward acquiring understanding. It's a matter of handling circumstances logically rather than emotionally. There are no clear-cut, infallible formulas for achieving that mental state. One must work at it, all the time.

In doing that you will uncover many ways to increase your power of understanding. But there are three ways to get you started right now in that direction.

BE TOLERANT

Simply endure conditions and people's flaky behavior. Learn to enjoy and find intriguing the life-styles, attitudes, cultures, races, ages, appearances of others. This seems like such an obvious attitude for being understanding that perhaps it need not even be mentioned.

Still, we may be compared to the congregation who heard the minister preach the same sermon on tolerance every Sunday. Attendance, quite naturally, started falling off. Concerned, the deacons of the church decided they should ask the clergyman to change his sermon.

Approaching him, they suggested, "It's a fine message, but the members tire of hearing about tolerance every week. You certainly must have many other things you want to lecture about."

"Yes, I do," replied the pastor. "So I'll make a bargain with you. I'll stop preaching about it when they start doing it!"

It's a gentle suggestion of the importance of actually practicing tolerance, recognizing and respecting another's beliefs, practices, diversities, and contrasts.

Why is it so difficult to do this? Why do people find it hard to accept the differences in others? In other parts of their lives variety adds interest and excitement.

It's the stream suddenly becoming a waterfall, a clover with four leaves instead of three, and the gorge creasing the prairie that attract attention and arouse delight. But what one finds fascinating about the landscape becomes annoying in people. Differences in others become displeasing, even frightening.

How strange that is. For people need each other for their differences! Civilization would never have survived if all the earth's inhabitants had been precisely the same.

At some time humanity will have to realize this. Continents, countries, religions, families, friends must stop feuding and fussing about being different.

Don't wait for someone else to start. Face reality now. Human beings are unique. No two are exactly alike.

Accept this. Be tolerant. Thinking about it and doing it are two different vegetables.

The Answer Is Up to You

Actually getting there, being more tolerant, might be like the fable that is told of the elderly mystic who had perfect knowledge and insight of all things. When asked a question, he had never been known to give a wrong answer.

One day one of the boys in the village gathered the other boys about him. "I have at last thought of a question," he boasted, "that the ancient Wise One will be unable to answer correctly.

"I have captured a small bird. I shall go to the Wise One with the bird concealed in my hands. I shall ask him if the bird is alive or dead. If he says the bird is alive I shall crush the bird in my hands and throw it, dead, at his feet. If he says the bird is dead, I shall open my hands and the bird shall fly away."

With that, the boys went forth to the place of the Wise One.

On arrival the boy asked, "Tell me, O Wise One, is the bird that I have in my hands alive or dead?"

The elderly sage pondered a moment and then responded, "The answer, my son, rests in your hands!"

So it is with tolerance. The decision to be tolerant or intolerant rests in your hands. For you have the power, to a great extent, to choose your thoughts. You choose to hate, criticize, and condemn. Or you choose to look above the faults and abrasive qualities of those you encounter; you look for good instead of the bad.

Tolerance, in a way, is simply accepting people as they are. They come with a lot of virtues and a few defects; some positive and a little negative, always some plus and always some minus.

Strangely enough, there is a tendency to expect individuals to be faultless. In one's mind is painted a picture of what the employee, marriage mate, or friend should be. When the person falls short of the expectations, the "perfect people picture" becomes scarred; anger and agitation result.

This comes as a shattering realization to newlyweds. The blissful spectrum of laughter, dreams, excitement, starry nights, and billowy hopes is suddenly bombarded with the crumbling revelation that the new-found mate has certain imperfections. The mutual exchange of envy, pride, selfishness, ego, self-pity, fear, jealousy, and criticism will distort the expectation. Emotions will be aggravated; irritation will ignite irritation.

Accept People As They Are

Try to accept people as they are; avoid casting them in roles of perfection.

Will Rogers said, "I've never met a man I didn't like!" He eliminated the need for tolerance before it even arose. He looked for only those characteristics in an individual that he could like.

It is amazing how deliberately some seem to emphasize and seek others' negative characteristics. A certain measure of delight and self-satisfaction seems to be received through faultfinding. It is an expensive form of pleasure, for it will consume and overcome the mind and block out any vestige of tolerance.

Practice looking for good in others. Remember that you can have only one thought on your mind at once; if it is a positive thought of another, you have no need to strain for tolerance; you have achieved it!

You are the one who will benefit by striving to be tolerant. You will be happier, like yourself more, and enjoy your relationships in fuller measure. On the other hand, being intolerant causes you discontent, misery, even sickness. You know these things. But perhaps you are not completely aware of the effect of intolerance on your physical powers.

At the point where you become provoked or irritated with another person, you have ceased to tolerate that person. When this occurs, you are actually burning nervous energy at a rate three to four times faster than normal!

On those days when "things go well"—when your thinking is positive, enthusiastic, and optimistic—you end the day feeling "good" and with a reasonable reservoir of energy.

In contrast, on a day when you are frustrated and upset with people—when your contacts with people have been abrasive—then you are completely exhausted mentally and physically before the day is over.

During human relations seminars I have conducted, I have asked members to write down the situations or people that are intolerable, that create negative responses. Here are a few typical examples:

"My husband paces the floor and groans while waiting for me."

"My wife's gossiping on the telephone."

"Coming home from a hard day's work and finding the house in a mess and no dinner ready."

"My supervisor's unreasonableness."

"People who make sarcastic remarks."

"A loud, constant laugh."

"To have to wait for a person who is late for an appointment."

"Lack of courtesy."

"People talking behind my back in unpleasant undertones."

"People who can talk only about themselves."

"Drivers who use the left lane of a highway at a rate of speed less than the legal limit."

"My spouse treats me as though I were completely helpless."

"Truck drivers who double park on congested streets."

"Gum chewing."

"People who expect to be waited on hand and foot."

"People not putting things back where they got them."

"People goofing off."

"Company that stays late on a weeknight."

"One who can't make a decision."

"People who are cheerful and talkative early in the morning."

"People who blow horns."

"My boss shows absolutely no consideration."

So these are typical situations that cause nervous energy to be burned three to four times faster than normal! Any of them seem familiar? Learn to concede and bear with these quirks in people without sour feelings, and you've conserved a lot of your emotional stamina.

Maybe the next two suggestions will help you do that.

HATE THE THING, NOT THE PERSON

On a warm spring evening in one of our major Eastern cities, a young Korean student walked from his apartment to post a letter. As he turned from the mailbox he was attacked by eleven teenage boys. He was savagely beaten and kicked beyond recognition. He died before an ambulance arrived.

Within two days the police had rounded up all eleven boys. The citizens demanded vengeance; the newspapers asked that the severest possible action be taken.

And then a letter arrived from the family of the Korean student. They asked that the greatest degree of mercy be shown the boys. The family was starting a fund to be used for the rehabilitation and social guidance of the boys when they were released.

It was their desire that the boys not be hated.

They, undoubtedly, through great determination and strength of will, were not hating the boys; they were hating the sickening characteristics that had gripped these boys.

They asked that the boys be saved from their brutality, savagery, hate, and sadism. They were even raising money to help. They were hating the thing—not the person!

Understanding people does not mean you condone all of their wrongful acts and undesirable characteristics. You will find it easier, however, to create an attitude of understanding if you learn to "detest the thing and not the person."

Conceit, selfishness, greed, cynicism, hate, lust, jealousy, self-pity, and egotism (to name a few!) are leeches that affix themselves to individuals to cause misery, sickness, and depression. These you can hate—but have compassion for their victims.

The personable, popular individual with no unlikable qualities presents no challenge to an attitude of understanding. The challenge is to love the unlovable. To understand the people who may exaggerate, show off, criticize, be sarcastic, arrogant, selfish, surly, or rude is a trial.

It is difficult even to want to understand these people. It requires self-determination to understand that someone has hurt these people. Someone has made them feel unimportant and unwanted—that they don't count. Let your defiance and prejudice be turned against those causes rather than the people who suffer from them.

Try this third idea as a way of doing that.

PLAY THE UNDERSTANDING GAME

Realizing the importance of understanding in getting along with others, there was once a group of us working at the same place, selling, who started a game to develop our attitudes of understanding. When we were together in public, one would ask why a person we encountered behaved in a certain way. Then the next would imagine answers.

One day we were on our way to lunch. The conversation went something like this.

"Look at those people lying around on the beach. Why aren't they working?" Then the answers started coming.

"They're firemen. They just got off forty-eight-hour duty."

"They've got rich parents."

"They're on vacation."

"They're recovering from nervous breakdowns from over-work."

"They've been told they have a week to live. So they're living it up."

"Let's face it. They're lazy. We'd be there, too, if we could handle it."

About then a young fellow driving behind us honked his horn and sped past us.

"Wow! He's in a hurry. Wonder what his problem is?"

"Just gotten word that his mother was in an accident. He's on his way to the hospital."

"He collects speeding tickets for a hobby."

"He stopped to help a lady fix a flat tire. Now he's late for work."

"Has a spasm in his right foot."

"Nobody loves him. Speeding makes him feel important."

"Wants to be a race driver. Just practicing to reach his goal. What's wrong with that?"

"Thought we were going too slow. Trying to tell us something."

So the conversation went. Of course, there were a few laughs that came out of it. But there was a lot of good, too. That crazy game did more to help us develop attitudes of understanding toward others than any stuffy academic program we could have taken. It can help soften the blow of resistance and rejection. I remember one morning one of the women came into the office upset because a good prospect she thought was going to buy had bought from another company.

"Why do people do that?" she asked. "What did I do wrong?"

"It's your lipstick, Joan. Try another shade."

"The buyer phoned in here yesterday and found out you were married. Guess that did it!"

"Sounds like a relative got in the act."

"They got a better deal from someone else. Somebody shaved the price."

"Competition probably used a blackjack!"

Before the discussion was over, it had become more serious. Which was useful. But at times, the humor and frivolity are just as helpful. A sense of humor helps in dealing with people. If you are going to analyze all your associations solemnly and soberly with unrelenting seriousness, you're going to lose a lot of sleep. Those why, why, why's? will pile up in your mind until you face everyone with a viewpoint of studied skepticism. That's quite a ways from understanding.

People are funny, interesting, fascinating, and lovable, and, like snowflakes, no two are alike. Our game of understanding showed that to us. Try it. Get your family, friends, or people at work involved. It will help you view people more kindly and acquire an attitude of understanding.

You will recognize the suggestions offered here for being tolerant are only ways of saying, "Have empathy."

Empathy is the ability to put yourself in the other person's situation. Great leaders, those who are notable successes in dealing with people, have empathy. They laugh with those who laugh, their tears are the tears of others, they rejoice in the happiness of those about them, and they suffer when others suffer. They feel the feelings of those they love and care about. That's empathy.

Having this treasured quality is important if you are going to make the ideas in this book work for you. Not sympathy, but empathy. Get out of your own skin and into somebody else's. Try to figure out what makes their hearts beat faster, brings them a touch of joy, causes their day to be better than the one before.

And, yes, you share the down times, too. Allow them to funnel your way some of the darkness of their moods and the setbacks of their hopes. You're there for them to lay off some of the heavy times and help them back to the lighter moments, even some peaks once in a while.

That's empathy, tolerance, and understanding. Look behind the shining disguises on those faces and you'll find hearts and minds that hunger for the understanding, empathy, and tolerance of other human beings.

They are affections that others need from you.

7

Listening Is Loving

"Wha . . . Wha . . . Wha . . . What are you doing to me?" stammered the befuddled professor.

This flustered, confused behavior was a reaction to his attempt to speak to thirty people who were busily demonstrating poor listening habits—yawning, talking among themselves, shuffling their feet, gazing out the windows, some even faking sleeping.

It was a set-up stunt rigged during a seminar on listening that I conducted at one of the Midwestern universities. During the morning break I asked the professor who was auditing the program to get some materials from the business office listing management courses offered by the school. I suggested that he explain the curriculum to the group immediately after the break.

While he was gone, I rehearsed the participants in about a half dozen horrible listening habits. When our "pigeon" returned and got to the front of the room, they were instructed to welcome him with applause, but as soon as he opened his mouth they were to fall into their badgering.

The poor fellow's reaction—the stuttering, wild-eyed, hurt confusion—was the most spontaneous and illustrative script of an individual's reaction to poor listening that I have ever observed.

"What are you doing to me?" he pleaded.

The words that spurted out were the ones that are scratching about in the hearts of the many who are confronted by indifferent listeners.

"What are you doing to me?" they are saying. "Listen to me. I have something to say! I'm important! Words and thoughts are thrashing about in my mind! I must let them out! They're me! They want to be expressed! Why do you turn away? Why do you ignore me, interrupt me, look at me with your narrow critical stare? Please! Please! Listen to me!"

PEOPLE WOULD RATHER TALK THAN LISTEN

Of all of the actions that can make another human being feel significant and worthwhile there is none more vital than skilled listening. Still, it is the most overlooked.

Ask some friends if they have any problems in communicating, and they will probably agree that they have. But only one in twenty will admit that the problem is listening.

This became apparent some years ago when I was involved with a course in public speaking in the adult education program of the Minneapolis public schools. The subject became so popular that we had to recruit two additional teachers to handle the people who registered.

Concurrent with these programs, over a four-year period, a listening course was offered. It was never conducted. Only a half dozen or so indicated any interest in it, never enough to make up a class!

Everyone wanted to learn how to talk! No one wanted to learn how to listen! Only a sparse half dozen had any inkling that listening presented any difficulty—that it is a part of interpersonal relationships that should be studied!

From a flat on Vienna's Bergasse many years ago came

testimony that talking about oneself and having another listen is not only comforting but, at times, almost lifesaving.

Herr Doktor Freud discovered that merely talking about one's inner emotions and the tangle of life's experiences can be healing therapy. Freud's therapeutic technique of psychoanalysis, letting the patient talk, opened a new era of psychology. Today, of course, it is the base for all counseling and psychological treatment of any sort.

PERSUADING REQUIRES LISTENING

OK. So listening makes another person feel good. What does it have to do with getting others to do things for you?

To answer that, let's look at people whose income depends on influencing others to act in certain ways: salespeople.

Let me start by relating an episode that occurred after a two-hour speech to 150 salespeople for a large West Coast company.

My plane was late for the engagement. I was picked up at the airport, went to the hotel, and got right behind the microphone.

After the presentation I was talking to the president of the company.

"Bill," I suggested, "I'll point out your three best salespeople." I directed his attention to three of the individuals in the room.

"You're almost right. They're in the top five. How did you know? Who have you been talking to?" he replied.

"I haven't been talking to anyone except them," I said. "I just picked out the three best listeners. I felt that prospects must have the same reaction to them that I did!"

Statistics would seem to agree.

A six-month study was done with one group of salespeople, all of whom sold the same commodity. Careful scrutiny was made of their techniques, habits, and personal characteristics. There was not much that was discovered about the art of persuasion, but one interesting difference was noted between the high ten percent as compared to the bottom ten percent.

Those in the lower group talked an average of thirty-three minutes per presentation.

Those in the upper group talked an average of only twelve minutes per presentation!

The ones that were barely getting by talked almost three times more than the star performers!

It's convincing proof that if you want to get somebody to do something, such as buy products, you do not "talk them into it" as the familiar impression implies.

I once heard of a salesman named Ben Feldman who had the reputation of being the most spectacular generator of insurance business in the country. I phoned him, identified myself, and said I liked to visit with successful people.

"Do you mind telling me how much insurance you sold last year?" I asked him.

"No, not at all. It was a little over sixty-five million dollars," he answered. His voice did not sound particularly impressed by the achievement.

But I was! "That's amazing!" I exclaimed. "I have friends in the insurance business who get their pictures in the paper for making the Million Dollar Roundtable. Are you sixty-five times better than they are? What's the difference?"

There was a moment's silence before he said, "I've thought about that myself. I believe the average salesman doesn't think big enough. Otherwise I just talk to people about their problems, work hard, and I'm the world's best listener!"

Those last few words, "I'm the world's best listener," reminded me of a real estate salesman on the East Coast whom I had met a few years earlier. His words suddenly came back to me. He had earned close to $100,000 in each of the previous two years selling homes. When I asked how he was so successful, he shrugged off the question with, "I really don't know. I'm a hard worker, and I would have to say I'm a pretty good listener."

Those are people who are stand-out achievers, ones who have stunning records of getting others to do things. And they credit their remarkable accomplishments to *being good listeners!*

Let's match that with our rule. *To the degree you give others what they need they will give you what you need.*

It becomes quite apparent that people like to talk, express

themselves, be heard. When allowed to do that with an attentive listener, they respond positively, favorably. They are open to doing the things the listener suggests.

THE KEY TO GOOD LISTENING

How do you become a better listener? It's so self-evident that there is an inclination to assume that it's easy.

You must *want* to listen.

You must lather up a keen desire to hear what the other person has to say.

Lukewarm listeners don't have an intellectual problem; they have an emotional problem. They lack the mental appetite for listening, either being vaccinated with a phonograph needle or so preoccupied with themselves that others' words are completely tuned out. So someone's ego gets clobbered.

But that's an emotional hang-up they have. It's not because they don't know how to listen. They just don't want to.

If you were compelled to take a course in parachute packing, you'd probably find it quite dull. Your attention would wander.

But if you were told that tomorrow you would be forced to pack your own chute and jump from an airplane, your earlobes would virtually vibrate with the strain of listening. Your life would dangle on being able to catch every word of the instructor's.

Maybe staying alive won't depend on your listening skill, but a lot of other benefits do. A fatter paycheck, closer friendships, a smoother running marriage, building ties of trust with your children, and becoming generally more successful can be some of the results of attentive listening.

TEST YOUR LISTENING ABILITY

No one can drive you to want to listen. Only you can do that. You might think you're already there. Let's find out. For each of the situations below, check the response you feel you would be more likely to have, either "A" or "B."

1. Your eight-year-old boy casually tells you the kids were lighting matches in the neighbor's garage. You think:
   A. Oh, my gravy! Did he light any? I've got to find out. This is the time to teach him not to play with matches.
   B. Let him talk about it. Ask about his feelings. Was it fun? Did they mention the danger? What did the other kids think?
2. You're all wrung out. It's been a bear of a day. You were up late last night, so you started out whipped. Everything that could go wrong did. Now you're mentally and physically exhausted. You greet your spouse, who says, "I've had a tough one. I'm really beat. It's been one of those days." You think:
   A. *You've* had a bummer? Let me tell you about mine! I know just what you mean. I want to let it all out. No one could feel quite as drained as I do.
   B. WHOA! I feel down, but maybe that other person is even more down. Talk about it. What went wrong? Anything I can do? Ask a few questions. Let the other person vent first, then I'll compare.
3. You are the supervisor of a department of a company that has just announced a new medical and dental benefit package for all employees. You've never heard of one that is more liberal. One of your subordinates comes to you and says, "I have a friend who works over at Klunker and Dunker. They have a program that's five times better than this one. Our company makes it sound pretty good, but they aren't giving us any more than they have to." You think:
   A. Doesn't this person appreciate anything? I've got to straighten out some thinking here. I'll go over the benefits again and pin them down point by point with Klunker and Dunker's.
   B. Why does this individual feel this way? There's more here than is being said. What's behind those words? There's some emotion of bitterness, hostility, anger that wants to be blown off. Keep the person talking. It'll come out.
4. Your twelve-year-old daughter comes home from school and says, "Some of my friends were talking about smoking pot

today. The teachers tell us it's terrible to do that. I don't see anything so awful about it." You think:

A. Oh, gracious sakes! Where did I go wrong? Smoking pot? My twelve-year-old angel? What will happen to her? I've got to talk to her right now.

B. She's opened the door. I'm being tested. She wants my impression. Be patient. Don't panic. Here's an opportunity for meaningful dialog. If I listen without criticism now, I'll be setting good roles for the years ahead. Let her go on. Why do the teachers feel the way they do? What do your friends think? Do you talk about it much?

If you checked "A" for any of the examples, you were displaying attitudes that contaminate listening.

Fears, prejudices, anxieties, preoccupation, self-concern, and the unbridled compulsion to talk all stand as roadblocks to productive listening. When those moods are in control, you don't come across as really wanting to listen.

If you checked "B" to the examples, you're on the right track. Let the other person empty out thoughts and feelings first. Then work out your own attitudes. You'll get more done that way.

GOOD LISTENING IS TOUGH LISTENING

If you see yourself as one who likes to listen, you might be thinking of social situations, the give-and-take chitchat that occurs when interesting little tidbits are being exchanged.

But the times when you want the other to change an opinion or behavior is usually tough listening.

Tough listening is when a prospect dumps a bucket of objections all over your demonstration kit. None of the objections have even a smattering of validity, and you have research and testimonials to prove it. Your mouth feels like a racehorse at the starting line. But the prospect has more to say. That's tough listening.

Tough listening is when one of your kids starts running down your value concepts, picking away at some of the standards that you feel are so vital to being a contributing member of the human race. You're inclined to blast away. The only thing holding you back is the realization that you'll be slamming the door on any future open communication. But it's tough listening.

Tough listening is letting a friend rip apart your glimmering political hero. You've got all the facts and figures to prove how wrong the friend is. But reciting your opinion isn't going to enrich the friendship. Listening is. Tough listening, that is.

Tough listening is getting the shaggy stuff out in the air in a love relationship. You're being judged and accused of some guff that you regard as unfair or untrue. You hurt. The first inclination is to hurt back. But that isn't going to help the other person love you. Tough listening will.

Tough listening is sitting in on the church's building improvement committee as they discuss taking out the dahlia bed and honeysuckle hedge and putting in a parking lot. You're violently opposed and are squirming with fifteen aesthetic, financial, and logical reasons why it should not be done. But lashing out at the other members, cutting their rationale to bits, won't put them in your camp. Studied listening and patient reasoning will. But it's tough listening.

Or maybe you're in on a planning session of some kind—business, social, or family. Your mind is popping with ideas and thoughts of what should be done. Every time someone says two sentences, you have an uncontrollable urge to slice in with a brilliant notion that's zipping along the veins of your mind. You perch on the edge of your chair, mouth half open, ready to jump in. You wrestle down everyone's efforts to maintain a free-flowing conversation. You win the talking contest but lose the trophy for stimulating creativity in others. You should have listened. But it would have been tough listening.

Tough listening is putting the clamps on that compelling anxiety to express yourself. It's a strain on self-discipline at times. Indeed, simply restraining your verbal velocity isn't enough. Rise higher to demonstrate the qualities of intent, active listening.

I don't have to tell you how to do that. You know. Look around you. Notice the traits of the people whom you enjoy talking to, the good listeners.

They show their interest with their eyes, posture, and the ways that they react. At times they might smile, raise the eyebrows, and nod their heads in agreement. It's a sort of indescribable mood that says, "I enjoy listening to you. You're important to me."

Although their listening characteristics are not passive, a calmness and patience about them is communicating, "Take your time. I have nothing more vital to do at the moment than hear what you have to say."

HABITS TO AVOID

There are a lot of things these people do not do. Fidgeting, squirming, doodling, doubting, disagreeing, finishing your sentences, or topping everything you say are a few of them.

Another is difficult to describe. It is a critical, doubtful, skeptical look that can't be explained by mannerisms at all. It's a coldness and chill in another's eyes that says, "I don't care about you. I question what you're saying and who you are."

And there's interrupting.

Since interrupting is probably the most common and abrasive irritant to a person talking, it warrants examination. I call interrupting "pouncing" and the chronic offender is a "pouncer." So, if you don't mind, I'll use those terms.

Pouncing is a spontaneous habit, a by-product of the disorganized peculiarity of communications. You see, people talk in a rather random, disorganized manner. They don't get up in the morning and arrange the day's conversation in a logical fashion. Thoughts are expressed spontaneously, flowing out as they come to the surface of the mind.

But this creates a problem for you, the listener. You have to pick up the pieces of thoughts, catalog them, put them in order, and capture the message. Sometimes you must cross reference, patiently waiting for the bits to form meaning. It's like putting a jigsaw puzzle together to form one big picture.

Fortunately, you are endowed with the facilities to do this. For you are capable of listening at about four times the rate at which people talk. You have a lot of spare time to organize mentally what people are saying.

Here's a short example. A friend is describing an event over the weekend.

"They went over to sort of mess around. Not many people were there, so they started playing the game. You know there's a place to play at Lakeside Park. It's plenty big for just cork ball. All you need is a bat and ball. Fred and Joan brought that. Pete, Jim, and Alice were there. Do you know Betty Long? She works with Pete over at Buckbeans. There were some others there that I didn't know. But we had a great time. Everyone brought some sandwiches and pop, so we just stayed there till nearly dark."

Rather disjointed. But the picture comes together after a while. Just wait and listen, then ask questions.

Or there is an alternative.

Pounce. Interrupt. Cross-examine. Top off the sentences with your own thoughts. Finish phrases. Nudge the words out at your pace.

That's pouncing. It might go like this.

TALKER: They . . .
POUNCER: Who's 'they'?
TALKER: Pete, Jim, Alice, Betty Long . . .
POUNCER: Who's she?
TALKER: She works with Pete . . .
POUNCER: Where's that?
TALKER: Pete works over at Buckbeans.
POUNCER: What were they doing together?
TALKER: You mean Pete and Betty or all of them?
POUNCER: All of them.
TALKER: Everybody just decided to do something, so we met to sort of . . .
POUNCER: Because you didn't have anything better to do, right?
TALKER: Well, no, not exactly. We thought the park . . .
POUNCER: Clay Corn Park?

TALKER: No, Lakeside. That's over beside . . .

POUNCER: I know where it is. Albert had Little League over there one year, and Hortense's Campfire Girls put on picnics there. Mention Lakeside and it reminds me of bleachers with slivers and hot dogs and ants. Whatcha do?

TALKER: For one thing, we got into a game of cork ball, and then . . .

POUNCER: Cork ball! I haven't played that since I left St. Louis. It's big there. Did you know I spent seven years in St. Louis? First time I ever got that stick in my hand I must have whiffed twenty-five times before I finally hit the ball. I had a friend there who . . . but that can wait. Incidentally, did just the four or five of you play?

TALKER: Well, no . . . who did I tell you was there? Did I mention Fred and Joan? And then some others I didn't know. Anyway, we, uh . . . let me see . . . seems like I was going to say something . . . forgot what it was. Oh, well, it'll come back.

You get the point. Pouncing takes the fun out of talking. It distracts, detours, and congests the spontaneous flow of thoughts.

Should you ever interrupt? Of course. There are times when it's necessary for understanding. But usually, if given time, the other person will make the meaning clear. If there are questions, hold them until the narration ebbs out, then ask for clarification. This not only gives the one talking freedom of expression but your final queries show that you have been listening.

DON'T TIE YOURSELF UP WITH SILENCE

Don't come to the conclusion that effective listening is being perched like a sphinx while another rambles on. Nothing would be more boring than two people doing that to each other.

Listening should not inhibit self-expression, give-and-take, mixing and watching, feeling and talking, the depth and joy of people using the gift of verbalizing to share their experiences and opinions. You're going to have to work out what's right for you with others. For example, you'll probably do more storytelling with your children than you do at the League of Women Voters' meeting. Or you would probably put forth a lot more idle chatter with the cabin crew if you were co-piloting a 747 on a red-eye special than you would with a friend who wants to tell you about a marital problem.

Situations and people vary. You have to get a handle on when you should talk and when you should listen.

Just be concerned about the other person's needs and interests. You train people to talk to you or not to talk to you.

If you give pleasure or gratification through your words or spellbound attentiveness, people will want to do things with and for you. It's important to realize that you can usually have a greater effect on others by the way you listen than by the way you talk.

Your conversation partner will experience satisfaction when you render rapt alertness to the conversation and allow it to run at his or her speed and tempo. When a person can be relaxed in your presence, letting out whatever is inside, pausing, thinking, skipping, starting over, stammering a little, going back and forth spurred on by the glow of interest in your eyes—that's great listening!

Learn to do that, and the world will need you. It's a way of caring. No, it's more than that. It's a way of loving. Maybe that's the most appropriate way of summing up this subject. Listening is loving!

8

Scratching People Where They Itch

Frank Bowman was anxiously calling a purchasing agent: "Just checking back to find out how I came out on that bid."

"Oh, yes. That order went to Northwest Products."

"But . . . I don't see . . . ah . . . were they lower than I was? I really sharpened my pencil on that one." His voice sounded puzzled, defeated.

"Well, no. Actually they were a little higher. But there were some other things that came into consideration."

When the conversation ended, Frank hung up, turned to his wife, and blurted, "I just can't figure out people. They say one thing and do another. I think there's some funny stuff going on here that I don't know about."

Welcome to the human race, Frank Bowman! On that same sunny morning there were a few million people feeling just as chagrined and baffled as you were!

There was the mother rebuking her daughter. "Were you out

with that Hayden boy again last night? I don't for the life of me know what you see in him!"

And the plant manager was confronting the night foreman. "What in the devil is wrong with that night crew? They don't get out one-tenth the work they should. And look at the mess they leave. They've got me stumped!"

And marriage partners are having at it. "I still don't know why you can't call me if you're going to be late for dinner."

"I explained that last night. Now if you want to argue, let's talk about the perfectly good money you spent for that goofy purse. You need another purse like you need two more feet."

On the same day a father was peering down at a sheepish-faced boy and impatiently saying, "Son, you promised me you wouldn't get into any more fights. Last night Billy Sawyer's dad called me again."

"Well, the rest of the kids . . . "

"I'm not talking about the rest of the kids. I'm talking about you and the promise you made me!"

Don't be too hard on the boy, Dad. He's not that much different from grown-ups. You'd realize that if you were to listen in on Jane Adams, the real estate agent, calling her prospects.

"Mrs. Devors? This is Jane Adams. I've finally found the house you were looking for."

"Oh, we've already bought a home."

"Did you locate on the south side?"

"No, we ended up on the north side. It's a little far for Albert to drive to work, but he thought it was worth it."

"I know you were looking for a one-story home . . . "

"Well, actually we bought a two-story place."

"If it's the two bedrooms you wanted, I'm sure they're . . . "

"This is four bedrooms. I know it's more than we need, but we just fell in love with this place."

"Well, good luck in your new home, Mrs. Devors. If there is any way I can help in the future, please let me know."

So Jane Adams puts down the phone, turns to the secretary,

and says, "What a way to start the day! I give up! I just don't understand why people act the way they do sometimes."

Don't be too deflated, Jane. Your lost sale was peanuts compared to the undoing years ago of Helmsley and Wein, two of New York City's wealthiest realtors. They announced through the press that a deal was set for them to buy the $150 million theater and hotel empire of seventy-seven-year-old J. Meyer Schine. Then, in the midst of final negotiations, Schine suddenly sold out to Morris Karp for $75 million dollars.

"If I appear calm," the delighted Karp told *Forbes* magazine, "it's because I'm still under shock!"

According to those close to the deal, Schine blew up when he read that Helmsley said, "Schine wanted to sell because he was an old man."

BEHAVIOR IS SHAPED BY EMOTIONS

And so it goes!

People often become confused and irritated when they try to understand why others behave the way they do. They make the mistake of assuming that others do things from logic, reason, and intelligence. But that's not true. Human beings act emotionally. And emotions defy analysis, judgment, and reason.

But they must be dealt with if you are going to influence someone's behavior. For human beings are emotionally directed organisms. We are intellectual, yes, but not intellectually *directed*. People are moved and motivated by emotions. Living is a constant process of trying to satisfy emotional needs and wants. Intellect and logic do not motivate. Emotion does.

When you want to get someone to do something, you must talk to emotions—not the intellect. Talking to one's intellect stimulates thought, but talking to emotions stimulates action.

How do you talk to emotions? Gently. Patiently. Persuasively. With empathy. That means putting yourself in the other person's situation, trying to feel as you imagine that person feels.

Sydney J. Harris, the columnist, once wrote:

"Thomas Aquinas, who knew more about education and persuasion than almost anybody who ever lived, once said that when you want to convert someone to your view, you go over to where he is standing, take him by the hand (mentally speaking), and guide him. You don't stand across the room and shout at him; you don't call him a dummy; you don't order him to come over to where you are. You start where he is, and work from that position. That's the only way to get him to budge."

Another writer, Ralph Waldo Emerson, would apparently agree. He was a man of great intellect in the fields of philosophy, history, and poetry, but he knew little about getting a female calf into the barn. One day, he was engrossed in this effort.

His son, Edward, circled an arm about the neck of the calf and Ralph pushed from behind. The more they struggled, the more obstinate the heifer became.

Face reddened, drenched with sweat, and his hands and clothing infiltrated with bovine smell, the great sage was on the brink of losing his self-control.

And then an Irish servant girl came by. Smiling sweetly, she thrust a finger into the animal's mouth. Lured by this maternal gesture, the calf peacefully followed the girl into the barn.

Edward grinned. But Emerson, intrigued by the lesson he had observed, stood absorbed in thought. He recorded the incident in his journal with this declaration: "I like people who can do things!"

People are like the calf. You can poke them, prod them, push them, and they don't move. But give them a good reason—one of *their* reasons—a way in which they benefit, and they will follow gently along.

It's like the farmer at the political meeting. The local party workers were discussing ways of getting people to work. After listening to the conversation for an hour, the farmer got up and said, "I don't know much about people and politics, but I do know that when we talk about getting cattle to the rack, we talk about the best kind of feeds to use."

To persuade people to do anything, you must talk in terms of feed—emotional benefit to them!

PEOPLE HAVE THEIR OWN REASONS FOR DOING THINGS

People do things for *their* reasons.

That's so important to keep in mind.

People do things for *their* reasons. Not *your* reasons. *Their* reasons! And those reasons are emotional, aroused by the ways they feel.

The story is told that when Michael Faraday invented the first electric motor, he wanted the interest and backing of the British prime minister, William Gladstone. So Faraday took the crude model—a little wire revolving around a magnet—and showed it to the statesman. Gladstone was obviously not interested.

"What good is it?" he asked Faraday.

"Someday, you will be able to tax it," replied the great scientist. He won his point and the endorsement of his efforts by using the greatest lever of human behavior there is.

Here was an invention that represented Faraday's sweat, toil, and genius. When asked what good it was, no one would blame him for describing his dreams, the imaginative uses, and his ideas of his invention's potential.

But those were his viewpoints. And he knew they would fall on cynical ears.

But, "Someday you can tax it," was the language of the politician. Now Gladstone had a reason, *his* reason, for becoming interested in the machine.

If you want somebody to do something, you must provide that person with a reason. That's the first step in the persuasion process.

EMOTIONS ARE IMPORTANT IN PERSUASION

You will have many day-to-day dealings with people in which there is very little persuasion involved. Follow the ideas in this book, and you will win their cooperation and efforts. They will do things for you spontaneously and willingly, often without being asked.

However, there are other situations that require persuasion. When people balk, resist, or have to spend money or effort, it may take some persuasion to get their agreement.

No surefire way exists for doing this. But when successful persuasion takes place, it's because someone's emotions have been touched.

Emotions are difficult to analyze. You probably have quite a tussle wrestling around with your own, let alone trying to comprehend someone else's. All we know is that emotions are a part of the churning forces within the human being, the wants, needs, moods, longings, and unsolved problems. Help a person separate just one of those unsettled urgings, understand and quiet it, and you have accomplished the persuasion process.

THE DAY I LEARNED TO SELL

I will never forget the day I uncovered the persuasion process for myself. It was after I had been on my first sales job for a little over two months.

I started out selling educational programs and was a horrible failure. I worked hard every day, even weekends and evenings, talking to people. Talking (that's all I did) about the wrong things. I told them how wonderful the school and courses were, pointing out in detail the contents and structure of the programs.

I enrolled two people in seventy-five days. That was done only because I sat and wore out the prospects who were already inclined toward the school before I got to them. Then I experienced the persuasive revelation that enabled me to fill every class in the school, enrolling as many as eight students in one day (compared to two in seventy-five days!).

It happened to me almost in desperation. One hot summer day, tired of describing the school and courses to people and being put off and turned down, I had one more appointment, which, although weary and worn out, I kept. I was going to get in and get out as fast as possible just to finish the discouraging day.

So I decided to chat with the young man, named Joe, for a few minutes, find out what he wanted, and turn him down rather than going through a lengthy presentation and having him turn me down.

So I asked Joe what he wanted in life. He told me, "Success."

We talked about what that meant to him. He thought about it. Visions of enough money to have a new car, clothes, savings—maybe get married—came up. The more we discussed those things, the more definite they became. He identified the kind of car he wanted, how much would be a nice amount to have in the bank, and what it would take to get married.

Suddenly, to me, Joe was not just another prospect, but a person, one that needed my help! I became more interested in him than I was in talking about the school.

I asked if he had a plan for getting what he wanted. There was none. Some vague thoughts, yes, but no definite plan. So we went over the possibilities. I shared my knowledge of education, developing marketable skills, and what it took to get started in a career.

The conversation swung around to the school I represented and how it would fit into Joe's life. Everything meshed. I left his home with a deposit on the tuition and a signed application to register.

I was elated! All of my stumbling and fumbling for the previous two months was behind me now. I had discovered what I had been doing wrong. Too much time had been wasted talking about the school, the teachers, and the material. But nobody wanted to buy those. No one wanted to spend time and money sitting in a stuffy classroom studying, working, while friends were out having a good time.

But they would do that if, in the end, it gave them what they wanted. As my knowledge of selling grew, it became apparent that my discovery was quite commonly known among experienced salespeople.

People don't buy a newspaper. They buy news.

It isn't spectacles that are bought. It's better vision.

Nobody wants goopy chemicals called cosmetics. But handsome prices are paid for them to bring beauty and good looks.

Millions of drills have been sold. Yet not a single person wanted one. They were buying holes.

People do not buy goods or services. They buy what those things will do for them.

That became dimly apparent as I helped Joe identify the emotions within him, sort them out, and come up with a way to satisfy them. He was motivated to a course of action that I had hoped he would take. I was also taught one of the most valuable lessons of my sales and management career.

Persuasion takes place by helping people meet their emotional needs.

LOOK FOR EMOTIONAL NEEDS

What emotions are we talking about?

You could study the sensitivity make-up of the human being for years and still not have all the answers. But that isn't necessary to sharpen your persuasive abilities. Why not start with the most accessible source of information—yourself! Chances are your general pattern of emotions is similar to that of others.

Your strongest desires are probably to be needed, wanted, and loved. Those take you into the cravings for affection, friendship, belonging, romance, approval, recognition, and a variety of other social needs. But along with those are your inclinations toward acceptance, respect, and being useful to others.

Of course you aspire to the goodies in life—fun, adventure, moving ahead, playtimes, inner joy and peace. Perhaps these are all a part of what you might term happiness.

There are nobler thrusts in your life. Self-satisfaction, fulfillment, achievement, the actualization of your uniqueness can play a large part in determining how your life is spent. Is this a longing for success? I don't know. Identifying emotions ends up in such a scramble of labels it's something like trying to summarize the dictionary.

You don't have to sort out all the feelings, put them into compartments, and then title them. Just get in touch with your emotions and know that what you have within you others have within them. Start there.

But specifically you probably differ. The intensity of individuals' emotions varies. Each person handles feelings differently. What turns you on doesn't necessarily warm another. Many would-be persuaders overlook that fact. They assume everyone is like them.

So the salesperson says to the prospect, "Here's just the tool to make your lawn beautiful and the work easier. Your yard will be the envy of your neighbors."

But the homeowner answers, "I hate yard work. I don't care what the neighbors think."

The employer beams to the employee, "We're making you the assistant manager of your department. There's a bright future here for you."

"But I was thinking of asking for a transfer," the newly promoted employee responds. "I don't like this department."

The spouse announces, "Surprise! I took what was in the quarter jar and put it down as a deposit on a vacation in the Bahamas next year."

"But I wanted to go skiing!"

So it isn't enough to be conscious of another's emotions and then appeal to them as you would your own. Instead, you must tune into a person's feelings and then try to get on the same wave band. Study the vibrations. Measure the energy and depth of the individual's inner stirrings. There are almost always a few simmering away that can move a person to action.

When you can do that effortlessly, sincerely, by habit, then you have acquired one of the basic skills of persuasion. It can be learned only by practice. Why not begin with those who are closest to you now?

SCRATCH OTHERS WHERE THEY ITCH

Persuasion doesn't end with merely finding out a person's emotional profile. Your "knowing" doesn't move another to "doing." You must scratch people where they itch. Search for emotions that are unsatisfied and then stroke those. Counsel people about what's bothering them. Then consider remedies.

There's a silly little story that illustrates that.

There was this fellow, Louie, who was having a terrible time. All day long his ears would ring and his eyes popped out. He went to see his doctor.

"It's that job, Louie. You've got too much pressure," the doctor advised.

So Louie changed jobs. It didn't help.

He got checked out by another doctor. This one told him the problem was caused by his teeth.

So Louie got all his teeth pulled out. But his ears still rang and his eyes still popped out.

Finally he consulted a famous specialist. After a week of tests the verdict came. "Louie," the doctor said, "It's bad news. You've only got six months to live."

Resigned to his fate, Louie decided to spend the last months in grand style. Selling his house and withdrawing all the savings, he went on a spending spree. He bought an expensive car, a boat, and a couple of tailored suits. Even the shirts, he thought, should be custom made.

As Louie was being measured, the shirtmaker muttered, "Sleeve 32. Collar 16 . . . "

"No," Louie interrupted, "Collar 15. I've always worn a 15 collar. Make the collars 15."

"We'll make 'em any size you want, sir," replied the shirtmaker. "But I must warn you that if you wear a 15 collar your ears will ring and your eyes will pop out."

Somebody finally analyzed Louie's problem!

So you're going to be the one who helps others discover what it is that doesn't fit in their lives and causes their "ears to ring and eyes to pop out." In other words, what cravings, desires, hankerings, preferences are rummaging around in them?

To do that, talk to them about their problems. Uncover their unsatisfied emotions. Find out what's bugging them. That's important if you're going to persuade a person to do something.

Because before you can convince another person to be happy with the solution you have in mind, that person must be unhappy with his or her problem.

That's vital! Don't gloss over that one. Run through it again.

For people to be happy with your solutions, they have to be unhappy with their problems! If they aren't, they won't act.

Now do you see why the lesson I learned from Joe was so valuable? I accidentally put it all together that day. The things he wanted from a career were covered—success, happiness, satisfaction, prestige, and future progress. But he got into them and made some sense out of their haziness. And as we did that, they grew in importance to him. In other words, he became unhappy with his problem. So when I produced a possible solution, he decided it was worth a try. He came to that conclusion, not me. There's a difference between that and jamming some proposition down someone's throat.

TALK TO POSITIVE EMOTIONS

Here's another point along that same line. You may have noticed that it has been suggested that you appeal only to positive emotions. Agreed that negative emotions are powerful in shaping people's behavior.

It's not uncommon to see someone take that approach.

"The bogeyman will get you if you don't behave."

"Buy these vitamins so that you don't get sick."
"What will you do if something happens to you?"
"Be good or Santa won't leave you any presents."
"Go to church or spend eternity firing furnaces."

Threats, intimidations, spreading doom and gloom about death, sickness, tragedy, and misery are all ways of playing on people's fears, doubts, anxieties, and insecurities. Effective, yes, but isn't that kind of a dirty trick? It's easy to alarm people that way. But it can also give them lumps of dread that don't go away. Is that what you'd like to do to people?

On the other hand, there's a warmth and glow that comes from knowing that a few lives are more joyful because you have sparked their dreams, ambitions, loves, and other positive emotions.

You may say that dwelling on people's problems is not positive. I have a story to share about that.

A few years ago I was reading a newspaper while sitting in a plane, waiting to take off. Unnoticed, a passenger sat down beside me.

Soon a voice said, "Are you gonna keep your nose buried in that newspaper or be sociable and talk to me?"

I turned to see a white-haired gentleman with a stylish goatee. It was Harlan Sanders, the Colonel of Kentucky Fried Chicken. I most certainly did become "sociable," and I had a fascinating time listening to the story about the growth of a franchise empire.

He described how he spent twenty-five years in his restaurant outside Corbin, Kentucky, preparing chicken for the tourist trade. Then a new freeway came in—seven miles away from the business. He had to shut down.

So there he was, sixty-six years old, almost out of money, no more than a sixth-grade education, and without a means of support for himself and his wife.

He applied for Social Security. When the first check for $105 arrived, he said, "I looked at that and told my wife, 'We can live on these for the rest of our lives or we can do something about it.'"

Then the words came out that I'll never forget. "I've found out that failure is only a stepping stone to something bigger and better. For behind every problem lies an opportunity if you just look for it."

Using his $105 check for a stake, he hit the road in an old model car to locate restaurant owners who would pay him a nickel a chicken for the herbs, spices, and methods for "the best fried chicken in the South."

That was the beginning of the happening that produced over one hundred millionaires and revolutionized the poultry industry.

The idea that buried within adversity are some of life's greatest treasures grew into the Horatio Alger story of the century!

The advice is profound. For the success of any individual or organization is founded on just one principle. A need is found and a way to fill it. A problem is uncovered and a way to solve it. That's opportunity. It's also the positive possibilities of persuasion.

Find someone to help!

Find an obstacle and a way to remove it!

Look for a challenge and how to meet it!

Find a problem and a way to solve it!

Find a need and a way to fill it!

It's a wonderful way to live!

Within that philosophy are the rich rewards of life. For to the degree you give other people what they need they will give you what you need!

9

What Turns People On
and Off

There are ways of communicating that arouse people's attention and excite their thinking. On the other hand, one can communicate with the opposite effect of building hostility and resentment.

Let's examine two of these opposing methods of communication. First, here's a way of communicating that turns people on.

USE MENTAL PICTURES

If you are appealing to the part of the mind that visualizes, you are motivating, arousing attention, and stimulating action.

If, on the other hand, you are talking to the part of the mind that analyzes, judges, and knows only logic, you are apt to be dull and boring.

Scientists have discovered that there is a little "hot line" running directly from the part of the mind that thinks in pictures over to the thalamus, the center of emotions. Mental pictures arouse emotion. Logic only helps a person to understand.

You need both to persuade. But remember that it's the visual characteristics of your presentation that spur another to action!

You've experienced that. You can read statistics about auto accidents until your eyeballs drop out. Nothing happens. But you can sit in your living room, close your eyes, and picture yourself in a horrible car crash and soon your heart beats faster and your palms get damp. Or pass by an auto accident where there are some red lights flashing, figures stretched out on blankets, and stunned faces gathered around, and you'll reach down to check that seat belt.

Here are several ways you can use the "power picture" concept to get other people to do things.

DEMONSTRATE

The old adage "A picture is worth 10,000 words" is no overstatement. A demonstration of any kind is of enormous significance in shaping opinion and behavior.

Want to teach your child to fish? You don't give the youngster a book on how to fish. Buy a bamboo pole, some line, a bobber, hooks, and bait. Then walk down to the water, assemble your gear, toss the line into the water, and put the pole in the child's hands. Now you have taught—by demonstration.

Can you imagine selling vacuum cleaners without having one for the prospect to see, feel, touch, push around, watch the dirt get sucked into? Do people buy perfume without smelling it first?

Whatever you're selling, find a way to demonstrate it. Whatever you are teaching, look for examples and ways you can present the material by demonstration. Look back on your education. Which have you remembered the longest, the words you read in the books or the things you learned by involvement and demonstration, mental pictures?

Dramatize. Demonstrate. Illustrate. Show and tell. Get the

other person involved. That's the way to add some punch to your persuasion.

THE POWER OF THE PARABLE

The parable is a powerful tool for communication and persuasion.

Thousands of years ago a slave named Aesop wrote a number of little stories, each illustrating a principle of life. The stories have lived all these years because they are fables, anecdotes rather than just words.

Jesus Christ was a great teacher, understood by children as well as oldsters, because he used parables.

A friend, Jess Lair, is one of our most successful contemporary nonfiction authors. His books, beginning with *I Ain't Much, Baby—but I'm All I've Got*, have sold millions. He summed up the enormous appeal of his writings once when he told me, "Communicating is storytelling. When I forget that, I become dull and boring."

Here are some examples that you can examine to check your own reactions. Study these alternative ways of presenting ideas to see which you find most interesting, compelling, and likely to capture your attention and cause you to think.

> The trouble with a lot of people is that they have no definite direction to their lives. They go about, day after day, in much the same way. They tend to follow others, but they do not have a clear notion of who it is they are following. This causes them to be in certain situations or positions to which they have been led by happenstance rather than by their own decisions.

That's one way of saying it. Here's another:

> Driving through a dense fog, a motorist followed the taillight ahead of him for almost an hour, letting the driver ahead do all the squinting, worrying, and road searching. Suddenly the red beacon ahead stopped and the two cars collided.

"Hey, why didn't you signal when you stopped?" yelled the man behind.

"Why should I?" came the reply. "I'm in my own garage."

People's lives are like that. They're riding through the fog, blindly following someone ahead, not knowing where they will end up. It's something to think about, isn't it?

OK. Which presentation had the most influence on your thought? Let's try another.

Psychologists say that your behavior is shaped by your concept of reality. This means that during your lifetime you accumulate your philosophy of life, the way you look at your environment, and what you perceive to be true and false about it. This will largely determine the way your existence unfolds.

That might also be said like this:

Two men looked out from prison bars. One saw mud, the other saw stars.

What do you see when you look out at the world, mud or stars? For what you see and hold in your mind will be what you experience as life.

Which do you like better?
Here's one more.

People go along from day to day, seeing only the same monotonous scenes. They travel the same roads, go to the same jobs, and follow the same routines they did the day before. They miss so much that way. There are so many wonderful sights they do not perceive and enjoy when they keep their attention focused only in the same direction.

Let's try saying it this way:

A small boy, walking along the sidewalk, saw a bright copper penny glistening at his feet. He picked it up eagerly. He felt a glow of pride and excitement! It was his! And it cost him nothing!

After that, wherever he went, he walked with his head bent

down, eyes searching the ground for more treasure. During his lifetime he found 296 pennies, 48 nickles, 19 dimes, 16 quarters, 2 half dollars, and one crinkled paper dollar—a total of $13.26!

He got the money for nothing—except that he missed the breathless beauty of 31,369 sunsets, the colorful splendor of 157 rainbows, the fiery brilliance of hundreds of maples nipped by the autumn frost, white clouds drifting across the blue sky in thousands of different billowy formations, birds flying, sun shining, and the smiles of passing people.

How many people do you know like that, who go through life so burdened with the same routine trivia that the magnificent adventure of living passes them by?

Which way of communicating was most appealing?

Persuasion is just another way of communicating. Storytelling can add impulse and magnetism to your sales talk, teaching, guidance of another, supervision, or raising of the children. Especially the children. They'll remember for years the stories you tell them, long after they've forgotten the preaching and moralizing.

Stories can be personal experiences. Don't drag them out as personal ego-pleasers. Stay away from your aches and operations. You are most interesting when you strip away the facade and disguises and disclose yourself as a human being groping for solutions to problems like everyone else. Sharing some experiences that helped you find yourself is immensely beneficial to others.

I know a man who cheated on his income taxes. Another fellow had to deal with his wife leaving him for another man. A woman had a drinking problem she had to face or lose her family. Those people shared their stories with others and had a greater influence than any number of lectures or sermons. They were real life parables.

BRING IN TESTIMONIALS

Of equal interest and more convincing in many situations are the experiences of others that reinforce your proposals. In selling, these are called "third-person testimonials." There is little that adds more to the strength of a sales presentation than bringing in the evidence of satisfied users.

There is a reason for that. Doubt, resistance, skepticism cloud the mind of the one being persuaded. A little voice inside is advising: "You'd say anything to get me to do what you want me to do. Your opinion or experience doesn't count." But someone else's does!

I have talked with salespeople who have said, "I don't know why I'm selling more now than I did a year ago. Doesn't seem like I'm doing anything different." In many instances it's because the individual was using a lot of customer feedback gained during the year as persuasive material to new prospects.

Ever hear parents talk about how much easier it is to raise children after the first one? In a subtle way, part of the reason for that may be that the experiences with the earlier child are used as guiding models with the others.

The same is true of managing or supervising people. The seasoned manager has all sorts of situations that can be recalled to help steer the activities and opinions of subordinates. They're impelling because they're real.

So much for what turns people on. Let's consider one way you can turn them off.

These are suggestions lifted right out of sales training literature:

"Keep in control by using questions."

"Inquire first and attack afterward."

"Never tell them anything you can ask them."

"Sell by asking questions."

I don't think that's very good advice. Questions can turn people off. I'll tell you why.

Everything associated with questions is unpleasant. That starts early in life.

For children, questions are the starting points for punishment, blame, scolding, and reprimand.

"Don't you know better than that?"

"What have you been up to?"

"Where did you go after school?"

"What's this I hear about you?"

But kids are not dummies. They learn to play the question game by shrugging their shoulders, making excuses, or answering, "I dunno," "Nothin'," or "Nowhere."

But with school the rules change. There's more at stake. Questions can mean shame, humiliation, and failure. Think back for a moment to how you felt when you were asked a question in front of a classroom of students and you didn't have the vaguest idea of what the answer was. You probably stammered, fidgeted, and felt stupid and inadequate. I know I did. It happened to me a lot of times. Those kinds of feelings take a lot of years to squeeze out of the mental system. I'm still working at it.

But what is even more painful is the use of the question by the teacher to punish. Taking out spite on some unruly teenager by getting the individual up to a blackboard with chalk in hand and then pronouncing sentence by saying, "Write down the answers to these questions," can be devastating.

The whole series of episodes is capped off in education by the final exams. More questions. More work, anxiety, worry, errors, and failure. But that's only the beginning. For questions have become a ritual in our society that precedes doing something unpleasant or manipulating an individual.

Lawyers cross-examine with questions.

Psychologists try unravelling the hidden miseries of the mentally tangled by probing with questions.

Snoopy acquaintances, with their brazen curiosities, embarrass the timid with their prying questions.

Sales people "qualify" or question the prospect before grinding in on the close.

Bosses "get to the bottom of things" by questions. That can also be a prelude to getting fired.

A doctor goes through the query and examination process before telling the patient an operation is needed.

The most unpleasant chore of paying taxes, buying, borrowing, getting a job, or gaining acceptance into any organization is filling out the questionnaire.

Even the word *question* itself is used to symbolize lost esteem, doubt, or frustration.

"How dare you question my honesty!"

"If there's a question about this, we should think it over."

"Why do you always question my reason for doing things?"

"I didn't like the questions he asked."

Questions are used to attack. Anger, resentment, jealousy, and criticism are communicated by questions.

"For heaven's sake, where have you been?"

"What time did you finally get in last night?"

"Do you have to act that way every time we go out?"

"What did you do that for?"

"Don't you ever think of me?"

Then there are those times when one feels a bit strangled by questions. You have a ten-hour day of exhausting, trying, frustrating experiences, at the end of which you are asked, "What did you do today?" Answer it in detail, and all the feelings of conflict and aggravation flare back up. Say, "I don't want to talk about it," and you're "not communicating."

Have you ever heard anyone say he or she had a lot of fun answering questions? Or a comment like, "I like my manager because she's always asking me the most interesting questions."

People are apt to find questions threatening, unwelcome, and offensive. They are repulsed by inquisitions. Everything about questions to which they have been exposed all of their lives has been unpleasant.

Teachers, bosses, police officers, salespeople, courtroom lawyers, parents, loan managers, and sometimes spouses use questions to probe behind an individual's natural defenses. There is an assumption that the questioner has power; the questioned, by the very interrogation itself, becomes weak and defenseless. So questions become identified with intimidation.

AVOID UNPLEASANT QUESTIONS

You don't need those sorts of feelings and reactions if you're trying to deal with people and get them to do things with and for you. This, however, does not mean you should not ask questions. They are one of the most valuable tools in communicating, understanding, persuading, and working with people, if you know how to use them.

By now you've gained certain insights into what not to do when questioning another. You can add these to the list.

1. *Don't ask a person why they do some of the things they do.* People don't know why they act the way they do. If they do know, they don't want to admit it. They'll cover up. So questions like these are threatening, offensive:

"Why do you act that way?"

"Why do you do business with Hokums?"

"Why do you work for that company?"

"Why do you say those things?"

"Why do you eat the same thing for breakfast every morning?"

"Why do you drive that kind of car?"

2. *Avoid trap questions, like these:*

"If I can show you how to save some money, would you be interested?"

"You want to grow up to be strong and healthy, don't you?"

"Do you feel a responsibility and concern for your family?"

"What do you think about people who have no consideration for others?"

3. *Don't force agreement with questions.* Queries like these tend to be a little conspicuous and conniving:

"Won't you agree that what I've been telling you is correct?"

"Don't you agree that if you buy my Zippity Can Opener your life will be much happier?"

"Are you in agreement that it would be to your advantage to consider your security?"

There's nothing wrong, however, with asking "How do you feel about this? Do you agree or disagree?" Always give the person a chance to voice differences of opinion.

4. *Avoid personal or offensive questions.*

"How much do you weigh?"

"How old are you?"

"What size dress do you wear?"

"Are you losing your hair?"

"How much did you pay for it?"

"Do you two argue very much?"

5. *Avoid baiting questions.* These are queries dangled before others just to get them talking and are so general that the answers could not possibly be of interest to anyone.

"What part of the dictionary do you like best?"

"How do you feel about the world situation?"

"What are some of the philosophies that you believe in at your church?"

"You read a lot of books. What are they about?"

If you want to get a conversation going, be more specific. Start with a couple of "small talk" questions.

Rather than thinking in terms of rules to follow when using questions, keep in mind the motives for asking questions. Don't ask questions to gain advantages over another or to maneuver, pry, cage, attack, or break down the defenses of someone as if the person is an adversary.

QUESTIONS CAN BE VALUABLE

Questions are marvelous tools of communication to understand, bring together, and move a relationship toward a common purpose. When used with that intent, they are welcomed as companions to meaningful interpersonal associations.

Be gentle with your questions. Start softly, letting the other person be only as expressive as he or she feels comfortable being. Let the relationship open naturally, picking up meaning and direction by casual inoffensive queries.

Begin by asking questions that are easy to answer. You've probably heard that you shouldn't ask questions that can be answered yes or no; instead, you should ask open-ended questions that make the other person talk. Don't get hung up there. Simple questions are beautiful to get a conversation going.

"Do you like blue?"

"How many employees does your company have?"

"What do you usually have for breakfast?"

"What are the ages of your children?"

"How long have you been with that company?"

"Do you like to watch TV?"

They can go on and on. They're light, interesting and part of the process of getting to know each other if you're conversing with a stranger. That stranger, incidentally, might be the person you're married to, working with, a son or daughter. Don't ever assume you know all about people you are with every day.

Ask questions that are enjoyable to answer. People like to express opinions but resent giving intimate facts about themselves.

People don't mind telling what they did; but they don't like telling why they did it.

If you find it necessary to ask questions, explain why you are asking. It helps take away suspicion and resistance.

"We're having a board meeting next week and are considering resurfacing the parking lot. What is your opinion about having the work done?"

"Your Dad and I are going to a P.T.A. meeting tonight to discuss some new school programs. I have some questions in my mind about them. I'd like to spend a few minutes and find out what you and your friends think about some of the things that the school is doing now."

My wife and I bought a new home. On the recommendation of a friend, I phoned a fellow about draperies. He showed up without a single sample. Then he explained that he would like to sit down with us, know us better, ask us some questions about our likes and dislikes so that he could do the best possible job of recommending materials and colors.

Two hours later we were still answering his questions and relishing every minute of it. We ended up buying draperies, furniture, and the whole decorating package from him! But he was a skillful questioner, making sure he disclosed when he first met us exactly how we would benefit from answering his questions.

Sometimes you can ask people questions just to stimulate their thinking. There's nothing wrong with that as long as you don't require that they give you their answers.

For example, are you turning people on or off with your communication? Are you trying to do things *to* them, or *with* them?

How you answer those questions could be the key to the way you're getting along with others.

10

One Sure Way to Get Somebody to Do Something

Marshall Field's mother once gave the University of Chicago one million dollars. At a meeting of the Board of Directors of Northwestern University, another Chicago area institution, the question was raised why a similar grant was not made to Northwestern. One of the directors of Northwestern was appointed to contact the Field family and as discreetly as possible uncover the answer.

The response from Mrs. Field was as candid as it was simple: "Northwestern never asked me."

One simple query, one small request, proved to be a million-dollar question for the University of Chicago! They bothered to ask.

There are thousands of human relations problems unsettled, products unsold, and tasks uncompleted that could be resolved immediately if somebody would just ask someone to do something!

The human mind is almost diabolical in its tendency to

complicate interpersonal situations that require someone to do something for someone else. For instance, read the advice columns of your newspaper for a few days and notice the number of problems that could be solved by a simple request from one person to another.

Many are like this:

> Dear Pauline Problem Solver:
> We've got this girl in the office whose perfume is giving us all sinus tremors. We've tried everything we know to get her to bathe in water instead of aroma of iris.
> We've opened the windows, moved our desks away from hers, put signs on the walls saying, "Ban Begonias!" started a fund drive for an air purifier, and last Friday all of us came to work wearing nose masks.
> She just doesn't get the message. Quick! What should we do?
>
> Signed:
> Perfume Polluted in Podunk

All the scheming, vexation, and conniving could probably have been avoided if someone had thought of asking the girl to use less perfume.

I have asked adult students in human relations classes to state one wish regarding something they wanted someone else to do.

Here are typical comments:

"I wish my wife would quit smoking."

"I wish my boss would give me a raise."

"I wish my secretary would stop wearing such strong perfume."

"I wish my neighbor would keep her kid out of my petunia bed."

"I wish the guy that rides with me to work would chip in a little on my gas."

And so it goes. But here is the surprising thing. I then pose the question: "How many of you have bothered to ask this person for what you want?"

Only one out of ten has!

They have pouted, sulked, intimated, assumed, flattered,

hinted, and hoped. But only one out of ten actually came out and *asked!*

Of course, that would have involved an encounter. People dread encounters.

A variety of unpleasant pictures are painted in their minds as to the ways the other person is going to react to a request. Indignation, hurt feelings, refusal, anger, loss of friendship, temper tantrums all loom as monstrous possibilities when posing a request to someone.

Any of those retorts could occur. But it's not likely if the request is made in the right way; the response could be positive instead of negative.

Forget your fears, timidity, concerns, and doubts about the ways people will take your request. Before you waste time worrying about the complex, subtle, difficult ways to get people to do things, try this one first. Ask them.

But ask them in ways that are likely to get favorable responses.

BE SPECIFIC

This one suggestion is apt to solve more of your frustrations about getting others to do things than any other idea. Just ask them as simply and specifically as possible.

Most people don't do that. Let's take the example of a boy coming to your door selling candy. He is likely to say, "Would you like to buy a box of candy for the Home Plate Little League?"

It's easy for you to answer, "I don't believe so." You're honest. You might enjoy the candy but you don't like parting with your money. However, saying no would be more difficult if the boy said something like this:

"My Little League ball team is selling candy so that we can play ball this summer. Will you please buy a box of candy from me?"

That's specific. It puts it right to you, making refusal a little awkward.

I heard of a milkman once who had more customers and sold more milk than any other route man in the city. He got new customers by parking his delivery truck at the curb, knocking on the door of a home, and then greeting the prospect with:

"My name is Homer. I deliver milk in this neighborhood. There's my truck right out there. I sell the best milk in the city and give the best service." Then, breaking into an ear-to-ear smile, he would ask, "Will you please buy milk from me?"

Perhaps there are more subtle ways of getting customers, but Homer's method sure worked for him. It's worth a try for anyone. Even around your home.

I had a habit of wrapping cotton around requests to my wife.

"Would you mind picking up my cleaning?"

"What would you think of going to a show tonight?"

Then one time we were having one of those soul-to-soul dialogues about our relationship. "There's one thing that bothers me," she suggested. "If you want me to do something, why don't you just come right out and ask me? You tend to beat around the bush. I like the direct approach."

So now I say: "Will you please pick up my cleaning?" or "I'd like to go to a show tonight. Will you go with me?"

She finds that more agreeable. All people are not alike. Talk about it with your family. You might find there's too much fuzziness in your requests to each other.

ONE WAY OF CLOSING A SALE

In selling, getting the prospect to buy is called "closing the sale." There have been books, courses, lectures, and training programs built around that one subject. But the most effective way of asking the prospect to buy is also the simplest and most specific. I learned it from a real estate salesman in St. Louis, Missouri, whose techniques had been seasoned and tuned by years of experience.

This salesman liked to smoke cigars. While his home hunters were looking through a home, he would sit outside, smoking his stogie. Then, when they made their appearance, he would inquire, "Well, how did you like it?"

Regardless of the prospect's answer, this question would come next: "Why don't you buy it?"

Then dead silence prevailed. What came from the prospect at that point would be an affirmative answer or a spontaneous expression of their inner feelings.

You'll notice he didn't say, "Will you buy it?" That would require only a yes or no answer. He asked, "Why don't you buy it?" There's a difference, isn't there? His question was a direct request for the prospect's feelings and thoughts and an honest appraisal of where everyone stood.

I shared this idea with a woman who had been selling real estate in Boston for four years. I met her a year later. She told me that she had used that question with almost every prospect during the year. Her commissions were three times what they had been any other year. Granted, she had not been too successful before. But at least it helped to get her selling career launched on a grander scale.

One afternoon I passed the formula on to Dan Oredson, one of the best insurance salespeople in Hawaii. The next morning at breakfast Dan told me, "Last night I gave my insurance presentation and then looked the prospect in the eye and asked, 'Why don't you buy it?' After a pause that seemed like an hour the customer looked back and said, 'All right.'"

I'm not suggesting this is a surefire, knock-'em-dead closing whammy. But I do think it is refreshing, honest, and specific.

If you're selling, try it.

Just ask every prospect: "Why don't you buy it?"

ASK FOR HELP

This technique was suggested to me years ago by a quaint, seventyish, petite woman named Miss Bee. She had a face like a cherub that had only two expressions, happy and happier.

One evening in a human relations course I was teaching the students were grieving about modern-day sales clerks. Examples were cited of customers being handled with indifference or actual rudeness.

Finally, Miss Bee spoke up. "I don't blame those poor clerks for acting the way they do. They are treated pretty shabbily sometimes. I always get wonderful service from the clerks. They are so nice to me. But I do have a method!"

And then she told us her method. "I go to a clerk, smile, and say, 'Will you please help me?' I've never had one turn me down," she slyly beamed.

Little wonder. It would take someone with a disposition of poison ivy to turn down that sweet little woman, looking up, asking for assistance.

But that's only part one of the Bee method. She went on to explain part two. "I quickly add that I know very little about the item I am buying and that I need the clerk's advice. I follow the same procedure whether I'm buying a button or a refrigerator. The salesperson is always anxious to help and gives me as much time as I want."

Airline ticket counters, department stores, hotels, taxi cabs, and restaurants are only a few of the many places where I've used the Bee Plan. I have worked out variations to it. The key to its success is apparently using the word "help" and approaching the other person with humility and sincerity.

"I need your help," is just as effective under certain conditions as, "Will you help me?" or, "I have a problem. Perhaps you can help me."

I was traveling from the United States to Kelowna, Canada, where I was meeting some friends for a few days of golf. I felt as though I were lost in the rough before I even hit the ball when my golf clubs did not show up at Kelowna with the rest of the luggage. A tracing call placed by the airline personnel revealed that my clubs were in Calgary, held there subject to certain customs formalities. I was told that they would eventually come to the local customs office, where I would have to file some sort of declarations.

I approached a young woman with the airlines who apparently had a certain amount of authority. "I have what to me is a serious problem. I need some advice. Would you please help me?"

"I'll try," she offered.

I explained my circumstances, that I had come to Canada to play golf and had a date to do so the next day. I finished my explanation by saying, "There must be something that can be done. Could you help me solve my problem?"

That wonderful person phoned over to Calgary and persuaded an individual with the airline to hand carry my golf clubs to the customs agent, comply with the requirements, and put them on the next plane to Kelowna.

Four hours later I had my sweet swinging sticks and the next day was gleefully slicing and hooking around the fairways with my friends, just as planned.

Thank you, Miss Bee.

Tucked in the corner of every human heart there evidently is a little of The Good Samaritan. To come to the aid of a person in distress quiets for a time this inner urging; a warmth, a feeling of self-satisfaction is kindled when an act is performed as an answer to the plea: "Will you please help me?"

BE POSITIVE AND POLITE

Maybe you're ready to try the ideas you've read about in this chapter. So you go to your teenager and say, "I have a problem. I need your help. The garage is dirty. It's about time you did something around here except pop your bubble gum and wear out your ear lobes on the telephone. Why don't you try your latest dance steps with a broom for a partner out there in the garage?"

You know what will happen. You'll get an earful of hostility and sarcasm or else a gallon of red paint will accidentally spill on your new car when the garage is cleaned. None of the suggestions in this book will work if they're used to cover up exasperation, sarcasm, ridicule, or revenge. To get the cooperation of another person, be positive, polite, and patient.

Let's take them in that order. Be positive. Hold in your mind the expectation of agreeable reactions from others. You are always communicating to others what your thoughts about them are. If your attitude toward an individual is saturated with resentment, dislike, criticism, or indifference, then get ready for a cool reception to any request you make. But when you approach someone with consideration, optimism, sincerity, and friendship, you will find that the temperature of the encounter will, sooner or later, be warm.

Secondly, be polite. Say "please" and "thank you." There's a raw feeling when you step up to a cash register and the person who takes your money then fails to say, "thank you." It's somewhat the same reaction you have when a waiter says, "What do you want?" instead of, "May I take your order, please?"

"Please" and "thank you" are all like caps on bottles of soda pop. Take off the cap and the liquid begins bubbling. Use the magic words; they make people feel more pleasant.

Never order or command another to do something. That produces the same sensations in another as scratching your fingernail on a blackboard—shivers up and down the spine.

Of similar nature are the words "You have to. . . ." Count the number of times you're clobbered with those words when traveling or moving about in public encounters.

"You'll have to get in the other line."

"You'll have to sign that first."

"You'll have to come back Tuesday."

"You'll have to fill out a form."

"You'll have to ask Mildred."

"You'll have to get the permission of your supervisor."

"You'll have to . . . " is irritating to many. Those words arouse resistance. People don't like to be told they *have* to do anything.

Replace those phrases with open sincere requests laced with "please" and "thank you." Your people business will chug along a lot smoother if you do.

GET PEOPLE TO SAY YES

Much can be brought to light about asking people to do things by studying those who do it in a flamboyant style with shocking success—the humbugs who bamboozle people into almost anything.

As a boy I would stand, fascinated, watching the road hawkers bilk the local residents at the Mitchell County Fair in Osage, Iowa. They went through a lot of spoof and hokum to wrench exorbitant prices from the spectators for cheap merchandise. There was always a sameness to their jargon.

They always started by building trust and training the bystanders to say yes.

"How many of you good people are residents of this fine county? Please raise your hands.

"How many have to work for your money?

"Do you like to save money?

"Would you like to have more money?

"Now for those people who said yes I have a gift. Step right up and get it.

"Now that's not all. I have another gift for you, but you must be willing to give up something to get it. I'm going to give you a quarter. But you must give me a dime. Will you do that?"

After a few quarters are given out, the pattern continues. The amount that has to be given for the gift gets larger. But the value of the gift gets less apparent.

What has gone on? Mark Snyder and Michael Cunningham did some modern-day probing to answer that question. They're from the Laboratory for Research in Social Relations at the University of Minnesota.

Selecting names at random from the Minneapolis phone book, they called thirty people and asked if they would be willing to answer eight survey questions for a public service organization. Only five refused. Another thirty-two were called and asked if they would answer fifty questions. This time twenty-four refused.

Two days later interviewers called the ones who accepted from the first group (twenty-five people) and those who refused from the second group (twenty-four people), identifying themselves as being from a different service organization. They also called a third group, thirty people who had never been called. They asked them all the same question. Would they be willing to answer thirty questions?

In the first group, those who had consented to the small request, nearly seventy percent agreed. However, of the twenty-four in the second group who had been subjected to the fifty-question proposal, only twelve percent agreed. In the third group, those who were contacted for the first time, thirty-three percent were willing to go along with the thirty-question proposal.

It's convincing proof that if you have been saying yes you will continue to say yes, and if you have been saying no you will continue to say no. And if you haven't been saying either, you're apt to fall somewhere in between.

Those hustlers at the county fair were ahead of their time! Besides putting the on-lookers into the "yes habit," they always got started with trivial requests and small change before getting their marks to part with the folding stuff. Again, psychological data shows they were on the right track.

A research team from Stanford University phoned a sampling of women. They asked each woman if six men could come into her home and identify every household product she had. It was added that the men must be free to look through every closet, drawer, and cupboard in the house. Surprisingly, of those called, twenty-two percent agreed to the request.

Another group was then called. Only this time the women were first asked a much smaller request, like answering a list of questions about home products.

Some time after agreeing to the simple requests, the ones phoned were asked to permit the men to come into their homes for the two-hour project.

This time over fifty percent agreed!

As part of the same project, the team called on homeowners, showing pictures of a house with a horribly ugly sign that said in big, sloppy letters: "Drive Carefully."

The residents were asked for permission to put such a sign in their front yards. Twenty percent agreed.

Then a different strategy was used. The ones polled were first asked if they would sign a petition supporting safe driving. After agreeing to that, they were later asked to allow the sign in the front yard. This time fifty-five percent gave their permission.

These and other studies seem to support a "self-perception" theory that claims that people are apt to act in a way that they have acted recently in similar situations.

START WITH SMALL QUESTIONS TO GET BIG DECISIONS

Start saying yes and you're apt to continue saying yes. It is also easier to make small decisions than big ones. People are more apt to change their behavior by a series of slight, casual alterations rather than abrupt, extreme changes.

Are you restless to change homes? Want to get your mate's agreement? What we know now about human behavior implies that you are more likely to succeed by suggesting that you both look at houses next Sunday afternoon and in other ways start thinking about it in small doses, rather than coming out with, "Let's buy a new house!"

Or maybe one of your children is flunking a course in school. You probably will get better results by becoming interested in improving the *daily* work habits than by demanding, "I want to see you get a good grade in that course!"

Or let's assume that during the morning coffee break at work someone offers you a huge, jelly-filled roll. You refuse. You're on a diet. Then you're asked to join a group for lunch. You decline. You don't like the eating spot. In the afternoon you get a request for a church pot luck supper and a friend invites you over for dinner on Saturday night. You turn them down. You have conflicts.

You get home that evening and are greeted with, "Let's go out for dinner." Chances are you'll say, "No, thanks." That's how you have reacted during the day in comparable circumstances. You, to a degree at least, have the self-perception of responding negatively to eating situations.

It would seem that the old adage, "By the inch it's a cinch, by the yard it's hard," applies to asking people to do things.

We often make it too difficult. Those bagmen at my county fair had that figured out. Or maybe it's just tact, diplomacy, and a little common sense. At any rate, before you overly complicate getting someone to do something, first try asking!

11

Why People Resist

Ask a person to stand erect, facing you, arms outstretched frontward, hands up so that the palms are toward you. Take the same position, placing the palms of your hands against those of the other person's.

Now gently start pushing. You will, in all likelihood, find the other person pushing back.

The individual is resisting. Through years of conditioning it has become a natural response.

People resist one another.

They resist others' love and friendship.

They resist ideas, opinions, and suggestions.

People resist attempts to change the ways they think and act, their habits, preferences, attitudes, and courses of their lives.

Children resist parents. Students resist teachers. Employees resist employers. Prospects resist salespeople. Marriage partners resist each other.

It goes on and on.

131

Resistance builds as human beings age; they become insulated from each other by walls of resistance.

Resistance is probably the most common barrier to effective human relationships that exists.

The constant realization of resistance impresses itself on the consciousness of people and inhibits their efforts to establish warm and friendly encounters with others.

Resistance impairs the effectiveness of people working together. It stunts the psychological growth of individuals. It narrows the potential dimensions of life. The range of emotional pleasures people could experience are dwarfed. Resistance retards the success of those in leadership or persuasive occupations. It causes people to hang back and avoid risks, and thereby suppresses career progress.

Resistance is the greatest frustration to the salesperson, an ever-existing source of emotional concern and conflict for parents. The depressing effect grinds away at the teacher, causing callousness and hostility. It implants distrust, resentment, and anger in the manager. Resistance can drive a wedge into a potentially good marriage, creating coldness, blame, and spite.

It can turn love into hate, friends into strangers, partners into enemies, cooperation and confidence into separation and rivalry.

To exist in harmony with people and win their cooperation, you must cope with resistance. That begins with understanding it.

If you understand why people resist, you will understand why *you* resist. Your resistance may be creating the resistance of others.

In your encounters with people you will always see yourself reflected in the actions and attitudes of others. Resistance causes resistance.

As one business executive said, "I never realized all the ways I was resisting others until I understood resistance. Even in my telephone conversations I was unknowingly building barriers of resistance. I find my relationships much more open and harmonious since I started managing my own resistance."

By knowing the most common forms of resistance, you will also realize why there is no single method for melting this opposition in others. It comes in various sizes and shapes, and each may require a different technique for handling. I have tried to take this big bundle of resistance in human beings and divide it into compartments that make some sort of sense, starting with this one:

"IT'S SHOWTIME" RESISTANCE

The world is a stage and all the people around you are actors or actresses. You see them in their roles and react to them accordingly.

I realized this one day when I was having a sauna in an athletic club with a friend.

The door opened and a rather portly gentleman with only a towel around his waist penetrated the belching steam and took his place on the wooden bench.

He was dripping wet as he came in, so I casually remarked, "You've been exercising."

"Yes," he replied. "I do my exercises rapidly, working up a sweat. I get more good out of them that way."

"I guess that's right," I agreed. "The veins extend themselves, becoming more effective in supplying the body with oxygen. The cardiovascular system strengthens, and the general muscle tone is maintained."

The man glanced towards me, nodding his head in agreement.

Nothing more was said until my friend and I left the sauna a few minutes later. He grinned as he asked me, "Do you know who you were talking to in there?"

It turned out that I had been advising one of the better-known physicians in the community!

Now capture in your mind's eye for a moment the picture. When you're in a sauna with your companions draped only in towels, you don't perceive them in roles. So I acted accordingly.

If I had walked into that man's office and seen him dressed as a doctor in the traditional white coat, I certainly wouldn't have offered him my dissertation on the physical effects of exercise.

The experience was a reminder that the roles in which we see others determines our response to them.

There are parts that some play that have always been customary opponents. Like cops and robbers, villain and hero, stonehearted landlord and destitute tenant, cobra and mongoose, some play the roles of eternal enemies.

So it's little wonder that in your everyday world certain individuals trigger words in your mind, saying, "It's showtime! On center stage front is this character before me who is about to do something to me. Put on the armor! Raise the spear! I must defend myself."

Classic is the image of the salesperson. Confronted with one playing that part, a recording clicks on in the psyche, saying, "Hey! I know you. You're all pumped up with this morning's sales meeting and a bunch of slick ways to get my money." So you crank up mental barricades that come out as "objections."

It sometimes goes further than that. You get downright irritated with that other person even attempting to sell you something. One survey revealed that the role of the salesperson was the one that bothered people more than any other. A whopping sixty-seven percent of those polled were peeved by the person trying to sell them something they didn't intend to buy.

There are others acting out their assigned functions that might be viewed as adversaries because of the roles they are portraying.

How about the boss, supervisor, foreman or one projected in the paternal image? Likewise, the politician of a different party probably gets a plugged ear and a few judicious criticisms.

Those who look different, dress sort of kinky, or are of another race or nationality may be viewed with a bit of hesitancy or suspicion.

An inborn trait that wavers around in most folks' minds from time to time is known as "sex hostility." It's a natural resistance to those of the opposite sex.

You see it influencing job promotions, friendships, employment situations, and even marriage associations. It's another form of role resistance.

You would probably resist a Communist; the newspaper has explained that they are something quite awful.

Cultural, religious, political, and social attitudes, together with conditioned experiences, value concepts, and habits, cause you to think of others in stereotypes, role images that stimulate resistance.

That doesn't mean it's bad. It's just the way it is. And resistance begets resistance.

For the next few days look at the panorama of people passing by and think of the ones you resist a bit because of their roles.

Maybe there's a bunch of them, simply because they come on as strangers.

You might decide that all that resistance piling up inside of you isn't really necessary. Life could be much more comfortable without it. We'll get into that later. But, for now, here's number two:

"DON'T CHANGE ME!" RESISTANCE

People resist change. They resist changes in their behavior, their habits, the way they perform their jobs, the way they relate to others, their life-styles, the things and people with which they surround themselves. People even resist changes in their plans, the day's schedule, or interruptions in their activity.

They resist changes in their thinking, their opinions, their beliefs. Psychologists know this as "cognitive dissonance," which simply means that it is almost impossible for the human mind to contain two opposing beliefs or opinions. People resist any idea or thought that might threaten an existing belief or habit of behavior they have.

This great resistance to change is very frustrating, because invariably it causes people to rationalize or justify why they shouldn't act the way we want them to. We end up putting labels on others' behavior when they resist us in this way.

In a marriage situation the other person is described as

stubborn, self-centered, or inconsiderate when he or she shows resistance to change.

In a relationship of love we accuse others of not loving us if they don't act the way we think they should.

We call change resistance insubordination or lack of cooperation when it is expressed by an employee, or raising objections when a salesperson experiences it with a prospect. It's bullheadedness in business negotiations or being negative or narrowminded when we see it in friends. We say it is immaturity, the wrong attitude, or even being naughty when we see it in our children. When the children see it in the parents, they say parents don't understand or "there's a generation gap."

"LOUSY MOOD" RESISTANCE

Seems like 150° in the shop. It's late afternoon. You're on a ten-hour day. The drill press broke down; the compressor sprang a leak. The lead man on final assembly slipped on an oil spot and broke his wrist. You're running behind, and every time you turn around there's an interruption.

You hear a voice beside you.

"They told me you're the foreman. I'd like to show you our "Miracle Meter." You attach it to a broom handle so that you can tell how many swishes your janitor takes to clean up. Here, let me get that broom and I'll——"

You glare.

"Go away!" you say.

Peddler Pete saunters off, muttering to himself. "Boy, what a grouch. Guess I'll bring my sales manager along next time to see how he'd handle that one."

Or a cold is coming on, your nose is running and your head aches, you've been overworked and underappreciated. Some kid is practicing drums in the next apartment. The catsup bottle just broke on the kitchen floor. The baby has colic, and the unfavorite sister-in-law is coming for dinner.

The phone rings; maybe she can't make it!

But instead: "Hi, honey! Say! Got to thinking. You know

Emily's coming over tonight, and as long as she'll be there I thought maybe I could bring Clarence here at the office and maybe we could call Henry and Thelma. You could just toss a couple more chickens in the pot."

Long pause.

"To be honest, I was going to ask you if we could call it off with Emily."

"Hey! What's wrong with you?"

It's happened to you and everyone else. You stumble around and mutter, "It's just one of those days!"

During those hours you'll probably resist any idea or suggestion that requires a decision more critical than whether to take one or two aspirin the next time around.

That's "lousy mood" resistance.

People have down days. They get depressed, discouraged, worn out, irritable. There doesn't even have to be a reason. Maybe they're just tired of others, the routine, the weather, or themselves. Or they could be sick, sad, or shaken about a bad situation.

Whatever the cause, they're in a grisly frame of mind and won't be receptive to anything except seclusion, escape, or winning the Irish Sweepstakes. Suggest something, anything, that requires effort or decision, and you'll meet resistance.

"WHAT'S MINE IS MINE" RESISTANCE

This is a kind of biological resistance to others. It seems to be true of all life. Every flower, every tree needs a bit of space in which to grow. In the animal kingdom each animal has its own domain it will fight to protect. Watch your dog's fur stand up if another dog enters the yard.

Human beings are not much different. Every person needs a bit of space, a domain, a little slice of the world to call his or her own.

People need their privacy and will resist any effort to invade that privacy.

The worker needs tools and a place to work. The executive

needs an office and has a secretary outside the office to keep people from entering. People will build hedges and fences around their homes to keep others away.

The urge for aloneness starts early in life. A child wants a room—a place of seclusion, perhaps, from the turmoil of trial and error; a place to be alone with stuffed animals, toys, and coloring books. A youngster builds a tree house in which to hide with secret treasures and exist only in a tucked-away, make-believe world.

There are dozens of indications that all have a certain biological need for bits of space in the universe and will resist the efforts of others to invade that space.

Studies have shown that people living in crowded, congested areas become more antagonistic and hostile toward others than those living in wide open spaces. People living in New York, for example, are apt to be less friendly and receptive to strangers than those living on the farms of the Midwest.

Is it any wonder that you keep the screen door between you and the salesperson who wants to come into your home? Or that the teenager is obstinate at the requests of the parent to change the kid's bedroom from exotic mishmash and hodgepodge to the well-groomed style of adult neatness?

I was conducting a seminar once at one of our Midwestern universities. Just before lunch we were discussing this tendency of the human being to defend one's own cubicle of space from the encroachment of others. I wanted an example to bring back after lunch.

I ate with one of the professors. As we sat chatting after eating, I took an empty cigarette package lying on the table, crumpled it, and put it beside my plate. In the next few minutes I reviewed a certain topic we had discussed and, quite unnoticeably, pushed the package across the table against his plate. I asked him for a reaction to what I had been saying.

As he expressed his opinion in the next couple of minutes he subconsciously shoved that cigarette package away from his plate back to mine.

It was not a conscious movement by him, but an inner voice

saying, "This is my little eating spot. I don't want your debris cluttering it up. What's mine is mine, and I'll resist anyone's threat to take it over!"

Biologically we all resist the attempt of others to enter our own little parcel of the world.

"YOU BUG ME" RESISTANCE

"You rub me the wrong way."

"I don't like the way you act or look."

"I don't appreciate some of the little things you're doing, like blowing your cigarette smoke in my face, touching me, getting too familiar with me, or using profanity. You're saying things I disagree with. You're griping, complaining, or criticizing. I don't want to hear about your operation or that your cousin has a friend who plays a better tennis game than I do."

"You're overbearing, you make me feel unimportant, your hair is too long, you wear too much makeup, and besides, you're redheaded and I had a redheaded high school teacher who flunked me in mathematics, so I haven't liked redheaded people since then. Unless you show me you're something other than what I think you are, I'm going to resist you."

Emotional resistance of this type is probably not always that specific or severe. More often we have only a slight negative initial reaction to some people because they have a mannerism, a personality characteristic, a way of expressing themselves or putting us down that is irritating.

Sometimes the scruff goes up when someone gets too tricky or cute with us.

Once I answered my doorbell and was face-to-face with a nice appearing young man carrying what appeared to be a sample case.

"Do you have children?" he asked.

"Yes."

"I'm in the neighborhood taking an educational survey. Could I step in and ask you just a few questions? It will only take about ten minutes."

I stared him smack-dab in the eye and replied, "You're selling books, aren't you?"

The poor guy looked toward the upstairs window, wished he were somewhere else, and stammered, "Well . . . uh . . . if we . . . a . . . find there's a need . . . we're prepared to discuss that."

"Nope. Not interested."

It was too bad that he wasn't more honest, because I was a choice prospect. I actually bought a set of encyclopedias two weeks later. But not from him, because I resented the humbug approach.

The same reaction is touched off by trap questions. "Mr. Conklin, if I could show you a way you could save ten percent on your grocery bill, you'd be interested, wouldn't you?" I'm going to find some way to avoid saying yes to that question, because I know I'm being baited.

Of a similar vein are those who would have one divulge one's personal business to a total stranger. I'm leery when asked how much insurance I have or, "Are you doing any investing in the stock market?"

My resistance comes out in the form of a switcheroo. I ask, "Are you? I assume you're selling investments. Will you please send me a detailed accounting of your personal transactions for the past year? I must determine if you've had the personal experience to handle my business."

Isn't that crazy? I know it's not a very mature way to act, but it serves a purpose. If you act a little bizarre, these people don't know how to handle the response. I've tried the customary ways of saying no. And they read back the customary ways of overcoming objections. So it's a standoff. They don't give up (they've been told not to), and I really have other priorities on my time. So I have to spring something they've never heard before.

Although these references are to selling, the same reactions develop out of other types of interplays between people.

You tend to build safeguards against the individual who "sets you up."

You can sense when someone is going to ask you to be on a committee or to make a donation when the conversation starts with "I was thinking about you. You're the sort of person that comes across as being concerned about community progress," etc., etc.

The old setup starts in many ways. Your children feel you out with questions to find out if you're in a good mood. Your mate, if you have lived together any length of time, has learned that your reaction to "How was your day?" should decide whether or not it's the best time to bring up some tender subject like buying a new expensive dress or going on a stag hunting trip.

Those questions that are laid on children, such as, "You want to grow up to be big and strong, don't you?" get about the same recoil as the old cliché, "Do you still beat your wife?" Answer it and get trapped.

If you ask questions without letting the other person know why you want answers, you can expect evasiveness, smoke screens, resistance. That's why the poll takers don't always get correct answers.

You do not get other people to do things by intellectually maneuvering them with tricky phrases and trap questions as if they were opponents in a chess game.

You do it by arousing positive emotions instead of suspicion, caution, and uncertainty.

Using force will meet with resistance. Snap your fingers, issue commands, and expect resistance—except with trained animals (maybe that's why they are so loved), who show little reluctance to follow the master's dictates. But people are different. Even children. Or wives. Also husbands. Plus employees. And especially people who serve meals at restaurants.

Go ahead and issue orders if that makes you feel good. But don't be surprised if the people on the receiving end do their best to make you feel not so good. Because that's the way you've made them feel. And they don't like it.

On the same wavelength is the rebellious little voice crying out, "I ain't so stupid as you think I am. You and your big words and fancy talk. You think I'm pretty dumb, don't you?"

Ever heard it inside? Aren't there people who make you feel insignificant, mule-brained, and about as tall as a pancake?

They have a sense of arrogance, superiority, or self-righteousness that dwarfs your self-esteem. How do you react? Probably about the same as all of the rest of us who have felt that way.

So you'll uncover some ingenious and subtle ways of resisting.

This could be carried on to exhaustive endlessness. There are so many ways that friction is created between human beings. Whenever it occurs, "Don't bug me" resistance puts a drag on getting things accomplished.

"I'M AGIN' IT!" RESISTANCE

You've met these kinds of people. They're against everything. They're negative. Turning their thinking to a positive viewpoint is like wrenching loose an old, rusty bolt. I'm not sure this book is going to help much in changing them. With some people contradiction, orneriness, and opposition are so deeply ingrained that they have become a way of life.

Antagonism, fault-finding, and being at odds with the world apparently serve some goofed-up needs that contaminate many sorrowful souls. They seem blinded to the fact that these traits are standing in the way of reaping most of the goodies in life. In some twisted way they get their jollies from objecting, resisting, and pointing out what's wrong with everything.

So resistance, to them, becomes programmed.

But we can learn from them. For there's a trace of that in all human beings. Negativism seeps into everyone's nature.

For instance, how do you react when you're driving down a one-way street and see someone going in the wrong direction? Honk your horn? Point to the one-way sign? Feel a twinge of smugness?

Be it ever so slight, and often unexpressed, there's a trace of the "Aha! I gotcha" syndrome in every person.

It means that people get a certain strange pleasure from finding the flaws and chinks in those around them. It comes out as resistance, a stone in the stream of cooperative behavior.

"I'M SCARED!" RESISTANCE

Fear inhibits. It looms as a monster blocking out all sorts of alternatives in one's pattern of living.

People fear . . .

> . . . danger
> . . . sickness or injury
> . . . making wrong decisions
> . . . other's reactions
> . . . failure
> . . . results of their thoughts or actions
> . . . change
> . . . exposing themselves to ridicule
> . . . criticism and rejection
> . . . loss of security
> . . . and a whole batch of other trivia too overwhelming to enumerate

There is one type of fear that should be emphasized, because something can be done about it. People fear that which they do not understand.

A neurosurgeon once rigged a person with equipment to sample the emotional responses under certain conditions of stress. When the words "I don't know" had to be said, the mind underwent a reaction similar to that of extreme torture.

So people avoid saying, "I don't understand you," and instead resort to some form of resistance.

What more can be said? Fear is a fact of life. Designed as an emotion to charge up the body to its maximum physical capacities (for dashing from dinosours and wrestling with tigers), it is now the primary cause of despair, disease, worry, and anxiety.

Also resistance.

RATIONAL RESISTANCE

If you try to sell shampoo to a bald-headed man or convince your wife to become a pro soccer player, some rather solid resistance is going to be encountered. A logical, realistic reason exists why the individual should not follow your suggestion. That's "rational resistance."

Now we come around to the interesting characteristic of this whole subject of resistance. Whenever a person resists, for any of the reasons pointed out here, that person will present the resistance as "rational resistance." And maybe it really seems that way to the individual.

Ever hear people talk much like this?

"I'm afraid."

"I don't like you."

"I won't change."

"Get away from my desk."

"I'm a negative person."

"Your arrogance turns me off."

Nope. All those feelings are wrapped up and hidden behind tidy logical reasons why the individual should resist.

That's the difficulty of handling resistance. You must develop a sensitivity to determine whether the objection is actually rational or stems from one of the other forms of opposition.

It isn't simple. But there are some positive ways of handling resistance.

All this discussion about internal obstacles in the minds of people makes them appear as rather awesome barriers to getting people to do things.

They are. Even the classifications outlined here are not all-inclusive.

You should realize from the variations of resistance and the depth to which it reaches in the individual that there is no formula for changing people, overcoming objections, or manipulating their emotions to fit your fancy.

But there are ways that you can help them neutralize their resistance so that it doesn't barricade the pursuit of a mutually meaningful objective. Let's move on to that in the pages ahead.

12

Dealing with People Who Are Against You

Here is good news and bad news.

First, the bad news.

People resist.

Now for the good news.

People resist.

And that's the paradox of resistance. It's both good and bad, depending on your point of view.

In the preceding chapter the tendencies of human beings to resist may have come through as pebbles in your shoes. Resistance is an opposing force to accomplishment. It appears as something that must be outwitted, battered down, overcome, or in some way subdued so that it doesn't wrap its ugly claws around a cherished purpose.

Those who resist appear as antagonists, ones who are depriving you or standing in the way of your intentions.

So your husband or wife, child, customer, employer or employee, social or business associate becomes one who is shutting you out from those things you need or want. You may feel frustrated, irritated, anxious, thwarted. With that cluster of feelings there is little hope that opposition can be dealt with positively.

Your success in handling resistance will be dependent on your attitude toward it.

There is an Oriental saying that goes like this: "If a medium in which you wish to create offers no resistance, there can be no durable impression."

When you place your finger in a bowl of water and then withdraw it, you leave no impression. There has been no resistance.

However, if you press your finger into a ball of clay and withdraw it, a lasting impression is left. There is resistance.

Only with resistance is there the opportunity for permanent change, accomplishment, noticeable result.

Look upon resistance not as a dreadful obstacle but as a friendly ally.

You need resistance. Without it you could not walk, hit a golf ball, write out a shopping list, or row a boat. You live in a world of resistance. It enables you to live as you do physically and build the muscles for work and pleasure.

What resistance does for the body it also does for the mind. It provides the force against which you shape your individuality. You grow.

Without resistance you would be a woeful wisp blown about in the chaos of life, a sponge soaking up the goop and guck of a wishy-washy existence.

Resistance strengthens integrity. Values are maintained, beliefs are constructed, and opinions are formed as a reaction to resistance.

You pursue ideals because you push away from less noble pathways.

You channel your efforts, steer your life, and guide your destiny because you resist dead-end alternatives. You harvest financial security, put together a career, and carve your own little niche in the world by your resistance.

You become known as your own person, develop uniqueness, and reap meaning from human relationships by resistance.

Call it spunk, determination, backbone, single-mindedness, objecting, resolution, stubbornness, strength, will, or a lot of other things, but simmered down these traits would come out as resistance. It's what makes you independent and free from being entangled and dominated by others. You're very special, the only one of a kind who ever existed, because of your power to resist.

Would you deny, criticize, or be hostile to that in others which is so precious to you? The ability in you to resist, which is so esteemed must be equally prized in others!

If you care about people, you will honor their resistance. If you want to help others, you will respect their abilities to oppose.

Loving another is recognizing that person's right to resist.

But if resistance becomes too deeply imbedded in one's consciousness, it can dominate thought and personality, becoming a restraining force in the total enjoyment and experiencing of life. It can inhibit the examination and acceptance of new ideas, choices, and courses of action involving change.

So ways of dealing with resistance should be known and developed so that we and those about us may be helped to use our resistance as a servant rather than being mastered by it.

Before getting into handling resistance, let's learn how to identify it.

Here are a few of the indications that the other person is pushing back.

VERBAL EXPRESSIONS

These are the most obvious signs of opposition. The following examples are well-worn sentences we've all heard or used at one time or another.

"Not interested."

"I'm too busy."

"Costs too much."
"I'll let you know tomorrow."
"Can't do it."
"Got to get more information."
"I don't have time."
"No."
"You'll have to see George."
"I'll think it over."
"It's not for us."
"Can't we talk about this later?"
"It's the wrong color."
"I'd never do that."
"I can't talk now."
"Don't like it."
"This is not the place to take that up."
"We've tried it before."
"Can't decide that now."
"Don't bring that up again."
"It isn't the right thing to do."
"The children won't like it."
"Mabel tried the same thing and it didn't work out."
"Can't rush into these things."

Companions to these are the voicings of shock or irritation.
"You did what?!"
"I'm surprised you'd suggest something like that."
"How come you didn't talk to me first?"
"You know how I feel about that!"
"You must be out of your mind!"
"That's ridiculous."

And so it goes. Words like those tell you that there is disturbance, disagreement, and restraint behind them.

SIGNS OF IMPATIENCE

Looking at the watch, wiggling a foot, tapping, nervously fingering an object, squirming, wandering attention, or any other repetitious movement showing restlessness are outward hints of inward opposition.

CONSTANT INTERRUPTIONS

Here we go:

"I'd like to suggest that we add the Uppity-Up hydraulic lift to our——"

"A lift. That must be like the one I saw at the trade show."

"Well, it would fit the——"

"Just a minute. I have to make this call."

"Our line doesn't have a——"

"Excuse me another second. Doris is waiting for this."

You get the picture. If the individual wanted to hear the message, the distractions would be eliminated.

UNRELATED COMMENTS AND IRRELEVANT QUESTIONS

You go to your boss to ask for a raise and end up hearing about Frederick the Great's battles at Mollwitz and Chotusitz without ever knowing how you stand on the pay increase. You've been told "no" by being led around the Tropic of Capricorn, and if you had persisted you'd probably have heard about Mt. Fridtjof in Antarctica as well. These people are quite clever at never giving you a direct answer but expressing their resistance by detouring the conversation in every direction except the one you want.

Realistically, a dialogue of this type might go something like this:

"I'd like to talk to you about painting our bedroom yellow."

"How about the curtains?"

"Well, I hadn't thought about those. Maybe new ones."

"Have you looked at any new ones recently?"

"Saw some down at Family Furnishings that——"

"When were you there?"

"Stopped in when I was taking Debbie to her guitar lesson."

"Say, speaking of guitars. There's a new clerk in the mail room that used to play lead guitar with Spud's Clodbusters——" etc.

So, we sure got a long ways from the yellow bedroom, didn't we?

IMPOSSIBLE REQUESTS

This is a favorite of parents. It comes out like this:

"We might agree to a motorcycle for you if you get straight A's next year, make your own bed every day, mow the lawn once a week, and earn the money yourself by salvaging pop cans and newspapers."

Or a business executive might put it this way:

"We'll consider that site for our plant, but first we'll have to have an ethnic profile of the residents within a ten-mile radius, soil tests down to fifty feet, prognostications of water and power availabilities for the next seventy-five years, and medical reports on each member of the village council."

The demoralizing aspect of this type of resistance is that some people believe what they're hearing. They go out and bust their backs complying with the requests, and after gargantuan efforts of accomplishment they come back and discover that the other people will say "no" in a different way. That's really what is being said in the first place.

GETTING ALONG TOO WELL

People wear masks. They are always disguising their inner feelings, some more than others. With many folks, old and young, you just never know where you stand. There may be hidden mounting resistance and then suddenly it surfaces, at times in a shocking way.

Some of the human situations that seem almost too good to be true suddenly fall apart. You've leard laments like this:

"Thelma was such a good wife. She never complained about shining my shoes, cleaning the garage, or working at the laundry for her spending money. Now I come home from a fishing trip and find out she's run off with the meter reader!"

Or how about this one:

"What did we do wrong? We brought up Roger to be a fine boy. Never let him be around bad kids, always in bed by dark, kept him studying every weekend. . . . He never gave us a bit of trouble . . . always so quiet and polite. Now he can't hold a job for more than a week, he's always fighting with someone, and he's in every one of those awful demonstrations. He just seems to be against everything."

The only way Roger has changed is by letting the resistance be shown instead of turning it inward. Probably that resentment and antagonism has been piling up for years but was well covered up.

Don't assume that because an individual is the model of cooperation, harmony, and agreement that there is no resistance.

Those associations are probably some of the toughest to deal with. Salespeople say the most difficult person to sell is the one who eagerly agrees with everything being said until the final close, when the prospect's jaw comes out, the glow disappears, and there is nothing in the air but a firm, irrevocable "No!"

Don't go into relationships expecting opposition, but, because everything's going ultra-smooth, don't assume there is not some of it there, well masked.

When you sense resistance, what can you do about it? First, let's consider some fundamental guidelines to follow.

EIGHT GENERAL RULES FOR HANDLING RESISTANCE

Watch Your Language

Don't use words that dictate to people what they have to do. They don't like to be commanded, herded, forced, or ordered to do things.

Ever find yourself snorting or fuming when you hear sentences like these?

"You have to fill out this form."

"You must wait in line over there."

"You should have brought that with you."

"You ought to think of this."

"Get that out as soon as you can."

Words like *should, must, ought to,* and *have to* are resistance builders. Commands touch off opposition.

Instead, ask for agreement. Use *we, us, our* in place of *you.* Get in the habit of using phrases like these:

"Could we get some information on this form?"

"There's a short wait. Do you mind?"

"Let's look at it this way."

"Is there something more we should consider here?"

Don't refer to objections as objections or resistance as resistance. Talk about reasons, ideas, thoughts, viewpoints, opinions, questions.

As you go about your daily contacts, be watchful of gruff, curt, irritating people who rub you the wrong way. Then make sure you do the opposite of what they do. It's a mystery of life why some folks work so hard to make their relationships unpleasant by using words, phrases, and mannerisms that are abrasive to others.

It isn't necessary. Be sensitive to the feelings of others; watch your language.

Be Likable

It is difficult to resist someone you like. On the other hand, resistance comes almost automatically to someone you don't like.

This entire book describes ways you can make yourself likable or lovable to others so that they will react positively rather than negatively to you. Admittedly there are other ways of getting people to do things. Force, power, intimidation, and use of fear, threats, and temper tantrums might be ways of getting reactions from others. But with those come resistance, reluctance, and animosity.

Positive persuasion is best. If you are admired, pleasing, and well-accepted by others, your life will move along much more handily than putting your relationships through a meat grinder to put them in shape.

Give Resistance Status

Make people's resistance a source of prestige for them, rather than humiliation. Maybe that's why they're resisting, just to feel important.

Reactions such as "I respect your viewpoint," or "Bringing that up shows you've had a lot of experience," will get you off on the right foot when faced with disagreement—much better, indeed, than "What has that to do with it?" or "That's really not important."

It's such a temptation to put children, marriage partners, and subordinates in their place at the slightest indication of opposition. Don't do it!

Encourage expression, especially of feelings. Then give them your purest interest and concern.

Let others' resistance be unique. Let them know they're very special. Don't say, "We always get that," or "All kids are alike."

Don't be too pat or nod your head in a smug, knowing way. The rehearsed response or memorized comeback carefully practiced and delivered with little sensitivity or regard for the resistance of another is a turn-off.

Don't Hassle

Avoid arguing, fighting, struggling, or any trace of hostility in your voice or behavior. People sense that. When they do, the battle begins.

You may have heard of the time-tattered legend of "overcoming objections" that is bandied about in sales circles. Nothing could be more damaging to your attempt to neutralize resistance than to do it by "overcoming" anything or anybody.

"Overcoming" implies conflict, the use of power. That is exactly what you do not want to do when handling any sort of a confrontation. Strive for harmony and cooperation, helping the other person make a willing decision.

Never disagree with another if you're trying to win that person to your way of thinking or acting. Always agree. There may be exceptions, of course. But if you'll go into your encounters always seeking areas of agreement, you'll come out right more times than wrong.

Never, never, never argue. You may come out on top in the argument, but the other person will rebel against doing anything you want him or her to do.

Don't Force Resistance to Be Defended

Probably the most common mistake that is made in handling contradiction is that people are placed in a position of having to defend their resistance. So it mounts in importance.

For instance, a husband says, "Let's take a trip to the moon."

And his wife replies, "Nope. The moon is made out of green cheese."

So he says, "That's a silly kid story. Astronauts have proved that's not true."

"I don't care. They didn't walk all over the moon. My daddy used to tell me that and he wouldn't lie to me."

That's sort of an absurd example. But you can see what is happening. One person points out how ridiculous the objection is, not being based on fact at all. That places the other person in a position of having to defend the myth.

This might be more common.

"Let's shop over at Best Food. The quality is tops there."

"Yeah, but they've got the highest prices in town."

"Oh, that's not true. Maybe on some things, but it's not that much more than other supermarkets."

"Listen, I look at the ads. I know. Let me show you a few examples from Thursday's paper. And if that's not enough, I can give you some comparative shopping studies that have been made."

So the concept of high prices has to be defended. Remember, neutralizing resistance is a thought replacement process. As long as an objection is being defended, it isn't being replaced.

Perhaps we could rescript that conversation.

"Let's shop at Best Food. The quality is so much better there."

"Yeah, but they've got the highest prices in the city."

"You're probably right. But they have fresh seafood flown in daily and the best selection of fruit and vegetables. Maybe we could just take a look. We wouldn't have to buy anything that you know you could get cheaper somewhere else."

You see what we're trying to do—replace the thought of price with the thought of the quality of the seafood, fruits, and vegetables. More about that later. For now, don't blow up resistance by forcing a person to defend it.

Don't Make the Other Person Wrong

You're shopping for a ballpoint pen and tell the salesperson, "I don't think I'll buy that one, because I read somewhere that it writes only 9,689 words without a refill."

"I'm sorry to tell you that you're mistaken. The company's tests show that 13,562 words can be written. So do you want me to wrap it up?"

"What colors do you have?"

"Red, blue, green, white, brown, yellow, and pink."

"Gee, that's too bad. I wanted purple. But thanks, anyway."

The salesperson proved you were wrong, and you found some reason not to buy. That's the way it is with people resisting.

The scripts go something like this.

"Aha! Here's the proof. I'm right! You're wrong!"

"OK. You're right and I'm wrong. But I sure ain't going to do what you want me to do!"

Trying to show that the cause of a person's resistance is false or erroneous is the biggest mistake people make in coping with resistance. An individual encounters resistance. The first reaction is: "Now if I can just come up with some proof or argument that there is no logical reason to resist, then I'll be able to convince this person to think my way."

It's looked upon as a kind of contest. Someone wins, someone loses.

It just doesn't work out that way. Prove people wrong, and you can be sure they won't do what you want them to do.

Prove your husband or wife wrong, and you can count on that resistance popping up in some other way, probably stronger and more determined than before.

Prove the error or mistake of a prospective customer, and you're on the way to losing the sale.

Prove that the boss bungled, and you've put your feet in mud as far as getting ahead on the job is concerned.

In other words, you might win the battle, but you'll lose the war.

If you're going to be successful in diluting resistance or getting other people to respond positively to you, then you should help them be right in as many ways as possible. Make them appear wrong, and you'll turn them against you.

In fact, this is good advice to use in all your relationships, whether you're meeting resistance or not. What good does it do to always be looking for the fallacies and inaccuracies in others' conversations?

You know people like that. They're always correcting others. Nitpicking is what it is. It's a way of putting others down. It's also a way of chilling associations.

I know a fellow who does that. Admittedly he's got the smarts. He has an ability to retain a wide assortment of facts and figures. He's forever pointing out the little errors everyone makes in normal conversations. But those having contact with him learn to deal with it. They avoid him or clam up when he's around.

The real price he pays for the little ego scenes comes with the close associations. He mentioned to me once, "My wife just doesn't open up and communicate with me. I can't get her to tell me what she thinks about a lot of things."

Why should she? The risk of communicating is too great. She's defending herself by silence.

Never correct a person unless it's absolutely necessary.

Don't Be Afraid to Lose to Win

Let people resist. Don't fight it.

You have a run-in with your teenager. You get your point across. Next you hear footsteps pounding down the hallway like cymbals on a tin roof.

The house vibrates as the front door bangs. That's resistance in action. Let it be.

Don't go chasing outdoors with smoke gusting out of each nostril and commanding, "You come back in here this instant! Who do you think you are, acting like that? I won't stand for that kind of behavior around here!"

Maybe you'll be able to subdue the behavior, but you'll get a lot more hostility shown in some other way. It's there. It's an emotion and has to find a way out. As long as it isn't damaging to the relationship, you can learn to handle it, can't you?

Remember Elizabeth Barrett, whose tyrannical father could not tolerate any show of opposition to his will? She buried her resentment within her, ending up a recluse, sick and worthless, until Robert Browning gave her the freedom and self-confidence to express herself.

She responded with some of the world's most beautiful poetry.

Perhaps fifty to eighty percent of all objections, resistance, and opposition that comes up in a relationship can be handled effectively by simply letting it be expressed and forgetting it.

Remember, resistance is not the same thing as "No." Because a person resists doesn't mean that the individual is not going to go along with you. That's often ignored. People are threatened by any show of resistance. They feel something has to be done about it. Not so. You can lose a battle and still win the war.

Let people pop their hearing aids, whistle through the cracks in their teeth, snort and fume. As long as they're not destroying the purpose of the relationship, what difference does it make?

What if your mate objects to the route you take and the clothes you plan on wearing, as long as you finally get to the party?

What do you care if old Baggy Pants wants to scowl and frown and complain about colors, prices, and the ink spots on your demonstration kit, if you wind up with a good chunk of his business next year?

And if the shoes are under the bed instead of in the closet or the records are on the bookshelf rather than in the record rack and the bottle collection is stacked against the wall when you think it should be on the garage shelf, isn't that OK as long as the kid's room is reasonably well kept?

Don't get too uptight about expressions of resistance by others. Let them blow over and then get back on track.

While you're doing that, don't forget the chapter on understanding and the sentence "I understand how you feel."

That's magic.

In fact, it's so effective in putting the encounter on an even keel that you could try using it every time you get opposition.

Use it and do it. Really get over into the other person's shoes and look at things from another viewpoint.

That's empathy. It's a powerful force in subduing resistance and cementing relationships. It's a quality possessed by those who lead, persuade, and find great meaning in their moments with others. They laugh with those who laugh, cry with those who cry, and feel the fears and apprehensions of those who resist.

But empathy is never acquired without the tools suggested in the next rule.

Use Patience, Ask Questions, and Listen

By far the most valuable utensils in neutralizing resistance are asking questions and listening. This takes patience.

It's difficult to sit back, listening with interest while resistance is being expressed. Most people feel the urge to debate. Most feel they have to "set the other person right" with the facts, "get some sense" into the head of the one resisting.

Think back, for a moment to why people resist. Many times it is only a process of asking for more time to make a decision. The individual is saying, "Slow down. Let me think about it. You're asking me to change or spend my money or do something I hadn't considered before, and I can't go through that as quickly as you're asking me to." So stalls are used. Asking questions and patiently listening will provide the breathing time necessary to eliminate the resistance.

These, then, are the basic suggestions in handling or reducing resistance:

1. Watch your language
2. Be likable
3. Give resistance status
4. Don't hassle
5. Don't force resistance to be defended
6. Don't make the other person wrong
7. Don't be afraid to lose to win
8. Use patience, ask questions, and listen

These recommendations are ways to prevent or diminish the tendency of others to be against your efforts or ideas. But they don't get into the basic skills of removing resistance as an obstacle to getting things done with people. The next chapter deals with that.

13

How to Neutralize Resistance in Others

Resistance is thought transformed into feeling. That's all it is.

Change the thought that creates the resistance, and there is no more resistance.

Most people ignore that simple truth. They battle resistance, trying to subdue it by proof, argument, and logic. They frantically seek slick ways to "overcome objections." How ridiculous! It's like trying to cool a room by putting ice cubes on a thermometer. The objecting, the resisting, is an emotion aroused by an opinion, a reaction, an attitude.

Your objective in neutralizing resistance is to help the other person alter his or her way of thinking. It can't always be done. If it is, however, it will be through one of three ways:

1. Replacement
2. Reduction
3. Conversion of resistance

163

Let's take a simple example and notice how each one of these processes work.

Assume you're in an auto showroom looking at a new car. You like it but say to the salesperson, "That seems like an awful lot of money. I don't know whether I can afford that."

You're resisting, aren't you? Now let's see how that resistance can be neutralized by a change of thought, first, by "replacement."

Suddenly, a fire truck roars down the street, siren screaming full blast. You watch it race past. For those few moments you are no longer resisting the car purchase. The thought of price has been replaced by the thought of the fire truck.

Let's examine the second process, "reduction."

When you express your feelings about the price of the car, the salesperson comments: "The purchase price can be paid over a period of five years with no interest or carrying charges. During that time you can be having fun driving the car."

Now the resistance has been reduced. The objection has been minimized so that it no longer seems as important as it once was. The advantages of driving the car outweigh the resistance you had to the price.

The third method of diluting resistance is "conversion." Using this, the salesperson would explain: "That price I quoted you is actually quite a bargain. You see, we're having a two-for-one sale today, and you get two cars for that amount of money. You could sell one car or give it to a friend."

Now what happened? The price has suddenly changed from a disadvantage to an advantage, hasn't it? You realize you'll be getting an immense bargain. Your viewpoint has been "converted" and your resistance disappears.

So those are basically the ways of dealing with resistance in others. They appear simple but actually become more difficult when you try working them into your day-to-day relationships.

Each method will be fully explained. I would suggest you try them one at a time. Don't become tongue-tied by dumping the whole batch of material into your dialogues in one day.

Pick out a point you like. Put it to use. If it works for you, keep it. If not, forget it and try something else. Out of the trial and error will evolve a pattern of dealing with others that will produce a greater amount of harmony and cooperation.

OFFSETTING RESISTANCE BY REPLACEMENT

Remember, our objective here is to replace the thought causing resistance with another that doesn't. There are a variety of ways that might be done.

Work Around It and Leave It Behind

On one of the moon shots a problem developed and there was a hold on the countdown. If you had been watching your TV, you'd have heard Mission Control announcing: "We're trying to find a way to work around the problem." A brief explanation followed.

Then the TV commentator appeared and said, "Well, that's it, folks. They're trying to solve the problem. We'll keep you informed of the progress."

Some time later the countdown resumed. Mission Control came back on and said, "We've found a way to work around the problem. Countdown has resumed."

Again the TV commentator reacted by saying, "You heard it, folks. They've solved the problem and they're going ahead."

You'll notice that Mission Control was talking about "working around the problem." The network broadcaster was thinking in terms of "solving the problem."

The broadcaster was reacting to an instinctive feeling within every individual that every problem must be solved, each objection must be eliminated, and all resistance must be subdued in order to get where you want to go with all of your relationships.

That's not true. Every battle need not be won to win a war. Neither do all problems have to be solved, nor all resistance quieted. At times you can do as Mission Control did. Simply "work around it."

Acknowledge the other person's viewpoint and keep going. The thought creating the resistance will be replaced by your continued discussion. It is important, however, that you *recognize* the individual's source of resistance.

Make a comment like:

"That's a good point. It's something for you to consider."

"You should decide how important that is to you when we finish our discussion."

"That sometimes comes up when people are evaluating situations like this."

"I hadn't thought of that. It may be a factor you'll want to bring up after we're through talking."

My favorites have always been something along these lines.

"I understand how you feel."

"If I were you, I think I'd have that same reaction. But before we make a decision, let's consider the other characteristics of the situation."

"I'd feel the same way. But let's look at it like this for a moment."

You may want to ask a question to communicate your interest. It lets the other person know you are not underestimating the resistance. The dialogue might come out something like this:

"It's too large," the customer says.

"How much too large is it?" you ask.

Or, "I don't like school," comes from one of the offspring.

"Nothing wrong with that. Want to tell me what you don't like about it?" could be your response.

"I don't want to go to Richman's for dinner if Jim Martin is going to be there. He rubs me the wrong way," your partner decrees.

"Can't blame you for not wanting to go, then. What does he do to bug you?"

In this, the simplest method of coping with resistance, make sure that you encourage the other person to fully explain his or her feelings. Acknowledge them, show interest, give the opinion full credence and importance, then keep going. If the objection persists as a block to the direction you want to go, the person will bring it up again. Then you can deal with it in one of the other ways suggested here.

Take a Detour

If there is resistance to.the road you're traveling, leave it, take a detour, and then wander back to the original path. Replace the individual's thoughts with a change of conversation, then come back to your proposal.

Here is an actual conversation I had with my wife. This was on a Wednesday evening. I asked her if she could go to a meeting with me on Friday night.

"Oh, I don't know. I have to get some shopping done sometime before this weekend."

"Well, let's think about it. Incidentally, this is a good hot dish. New recipe, isn't it?"

"Yes. That's one of Helen's. She was telling me about it, so I decided to try it."

"How is she?"

"Oh, fine. She was a little under the weather last week, but she's OK now."

"When did you talk to her?"

"Yesterday."

"Well, good. Glad to hear she's all right. Oh, how about that meeting? Do you think you could work it out to go with me?"

"I think I could. Do you have to know right now?"

"They would like to find out how many are coming. Why don't I tell them you'll be there and then you can cancel out if something comes up?"

"I suppose that would be all right."

Notice that when the spontaneous resistance arose, the conversation was detoured away to something else. When the subject came up again later, the feeling of opposition was almost completely diluted.

If you've been close to someone for a long period of time, you know the dialogue could have gone something like this:

"Can you go to that meeting with me on Friday night?"

"Oh, I don't know. I have to get some shopping done sometime before this weekend."

"Well, you don't have to do it on Friday night. You've got all day Thursday and all day Friday to shop."

"Listen, you don't know how many things I have to do. I'm trying to get that skirt cut out. Julie has flute lessons tomorrow afternoon. I've got to get off a note to Jane and Grady. I told your mother I would drop over there. The house has to get cleaned——"

If I had challenged her resistance, it would not have been difficult for her to defend her point of view by proving she was going to be busier than ten puppies in a butcher shop. As it was, there was no disagreement, just casual thought replacement that softened the initial opposition.

Pay a Compliment

You'll be amazed how a word of praise or a compliment, even about the objection itself, can replace thoughts of resistance with thoughts of agreement.

I knew a home builder once, Carl Fransen, who got out of the business of building homes and into the business of just selling them. He was good at it, too.

It was years ago that he taught me about handling resistance with a compliment. He told me about a sale he had made a week before. He was holding a home open for inspection when a couple walked in the front door. The man opened the conversation with, "There must be some settling here. I notice the front door stoop has a little separation from the home."

Carl said, "Could be," and then started showing them the home. In every room the prospect made some critical comment about the construction or design of the home.

Ending up in the basement, the man noted that the B.T.U.'s of the furnace were inadequate and the widths of the joists were too small.

Back upstairs, Carl asked the critic, "Are you a builder?"

"No."

"Well, I used to be," Carl said. "I know home construction and I have never met a prospective home buyer who knows as much about home construction as you do. You have obviously made a study of it. I wish every prospect knew as much about homes as you do. It would certainly make our jobs a lot easier."

Then he started pointing out some of the good features of the home. This time through, the prospect was agreeing with the home's advantages. He had made his point. He was an expert.

Before the couple left the home, Carl had received a signed offer to buy the property, which he subsequently negotiated with the seller.

What a master!

He could have used his years of experience and knowledge to put down every criticism that the prospect presented about the house. But the sale would never have been made!

Instead, Carl used to advantage his professional wisdom to replace, in the other person's mind, thoughts of resistance with thoughts of personal satisfaction. With that, all the objections melted away and the result was a sale, the harmonious conclusion of the relationship.

Talk Benefit

Replace thoughts of resistance with thoughts of fun, adventure, pleasure, enjoyment, recognition, prestige, and satisfaction.

People do things for emotional reasons. Resistance is emotion. It's difficult to dilute it by logic. But you can replace it with positive emotions, benefits.

To do this, acknowledge the resistance as suggested previously. Then talk benefits. In fact, it's a good idea to save your most powerful benefits for this stage of your dialogue.

Most people don't do this. They get impatient. They bury others with a barrage of advantages at the beginning of the conversation. Then there's nothing left.

You should know where you stand with the other person

before you start presenting your viewpoint. Probe, ask questions, get the other person to talk and express his or her feelings. Then start presenting emotional benefits.

Let's see how that would work in a wrong and right situation. First the wrong.

WIFE: You told me you'd take my sewing machine to be checked. I'd like to get that done. On the way we could look at those new golf clubs you've been wanting to see.

HUSBAND: Couldn't we do that later? I've got a lot to do right now.

Where do you go from here?
The big blast (golf clubs) has already been fired.
How about trying it this way?

WIFE: How would you feel about taking my sewing machine to be checked now? Are you busy?

HUSBAND: I really am. Couldn't we do that later?

WIFE: I suppose we could. I know you have a lot to do. But I thought we might stop on the way and look at those new golf clubs you were talking about. What's the advantage over the ones you have now?

HUSBAND: They have lighter shafts and special weighting in the head to make the sweet spot larger.

WIFE: The way you enjoy your golf, you should consider them. You've got the whole season ahead. It wouldn't take very long if we went right now. I'd like to have you show them to me. Might be something we could consider for Father's Day.

THE DUFFER: Let's go!

THE TACTICIAN: Oh, don't forget the sewing machine!

NEUTRALIZING RESISTANCE BY REDUCTION

Reduction, the second principle for diluting resistance, is a way of modifying the intensity of the opposition. Throw a little water on the fire; pack the red-hot coals of resistance in ice.

In doing this you don't eliminate the resistance, but you make it seem smaller, of little consequence. You remove it as the gigantic obstacle to the direction you're going with another.

Here are some ideas for doing that:

Exaggerate the Cause of Resistance

Man's Search for Meaning is a fascinating book written by an Austrian psychologist, Viktor E. Frankl. In it he describes the inhuman experiences he encountered as a prisoner in Nazi prison camps. As brutal as they were, he found meaning in them and his existence.

When free, he developed a philosophy of psychology he termed "logo therapy." *Logos* is a Greek word that might translate into "meaning." It's a system of looking at life squarely—not running from the torments but, rather, enduring them, even finding meaning within them. Phobias and neuroses may be deliberately emphasized to assure the individual that life can be experienced fully in spite of its problems. Sleeplessness might be handled by encouraging the patient to try to stay awake as long as possible.

Resistance in another can often be quieted in much the same way. Don't run from it or try to handle it all. Dwell on it, exaggerate its consequence, and then let the other person determine its importance. It's a way of saying that resistance is reality, but is it going to hold us back from venturing forth, trying something different?

A person says, "You want us to go to Middlebury, but the road there is a mess. I don't like it."

So you say, "Tell me what you don't like about it."

"It's bumpy, crooked, and narrow, with detours, stop signs, and potholes you can get lost in."

"Is that all?"

"Isn't that enough?"

"It's enough to tell me that you hate the road, and that won't change. But does that mean we'll never go to Middlebury?"

"Well, I didn't say that."

In a way, this method is something like blowing up a balloon until it bursts. Once you're on the course, you have to stick with it. Don't leave the balloon half full; it'll just keep floating around.

I was once involved in a discussion with a manager in one of our sales divisions about incentive payments to salespeople. He was violently opposed to a certain method we had adopted of doing that.

We started talking about his opinion. Each point he brought up, I asked him to enlarge on. He said that a lot of the people felt the same way he did.

"How many? Can you tell me which ones?"

"Well, for example, there was this conversation I had with one of the guys who was very upset."

"What was said?" I asked.

So he started. First, what the other fellow said. Then I asked, "And what did you say?" followed by, "And what did he say?" and then back to, "And what did you say?" and "What did he say?"

This type of specific, magnified discussion went on for nearly two hours. Never once did I present the company reasoning or try to refute his judgment.

But finally he said, "You know, I think we're spending too much time talking about this. Maybe it's not as important as I thought. I can live with it while we're trying it. I appreciate the time you've taken to listen to me. I feel better about it now."

"Glad to do it," I responded. "Your opinions are important to us. Why don't we give this program our best efforts, see how it goes, and then you and I can visit about it later."

"OK. Great. Thanks again." And he was on his way.

Poor man's logo therapy. Find meaning in the resistance. Dwell on it, puff it up, talk it out, and it comes out as a paper giant—something that is not as monstrous as it was believed to be and certainly not an obstruction to the forward motion of the relationship.

A word of caution. You might say, "Dwelling on the cause of resistance like this will only build it up in the other person's mind and it will become more important than it really is."

That's a possibility. You might use this idea sparingly until you're well grounded in sensitivity and confidence in handling resistance. It's like a lot of other suggestions in this book. None of them work every time in every situation. If they did, human relations and problems would be reduced to simple formulas, which they aren't.

Try exaggerating the cause of resistance. If it isn't effective for you, go on to something else, like:

Reducing Resistance by Comparison

Nothing complicated about this one. You reduce the resistance in the other person's mind by comparing it to a much greater cause of resistance.

"I just dread going to the doctor to have this corn on my toe removed. I keep putting it off."

"Can't blame you. Cousin Charlie felt the same way before he had his leg amputated."

I recently shopped for a new car. "When can I get delivery?" I asked.

"It's running about four weeks," the salesman answered.

"Four weeks! I can't wait that long. I wanted it for a trip."

"I know how you feel. But remember that other model you were looking at? That takes up to three months, sometimes even longer."

"You mean people wait three months for a new car?"

"Some do." He smiled.

"Well, I guess if some wait for three months, I can put up with four weeks."

You'll find lots of ways to use this bit. It's quick and easy, a sort of first trial when resistance shows up.

"You mean you're grounding me for a full week just for being one hour late for dinner?"

"I understand how you feel. But I hear your friend Jenny got two weeks for the same thing."

Or, "This price is out of sight!"

"I agree with you. But if you think that's bad, let's take a minute and compare it with a few of the other items in the line."

How about, "You want me to work all day Saturday?!"

"I realize it's asking a lot. But some are putting in every evening, too."

This method of coping with resistance might be like the fellow who asked the dentist how much it would cost to have a tooth pulled.

"Fifty dollars," was the reply.

"That's a lot of money for ten seconds' work," the man complained.

So the dentist suggested, "Well, if you'd like, sir, I can take longer!"

Reducing Resistance by Comfort

"Are you ready for this? Want to sit down first?" Those words have more truth than humor.

It's been found that people have less resistance when they're sitting than when they're standing. They have the least resistance when they're lying down.

You're not going to get everyone to lie down when they show resistance, but you can make sure discomfort doesn't enlarge their opposition.

If you're playing golf with a client and the poor person is five holes down with six to go, it's 100 degrees in the shade, and your guest starts huffing and puffing about your late deliveries, wait until you're comfortably sipping refreshments in the air-conditioned clubhouse after the game until you respond to the resistance.

If the other person is uncomfortable—tired, hot, cold, standing, worn out, or simply tense with the anxiety of the moment—the resistance can be reduced by putting the person at ease.

"Let's sleep on it. Things won't seem so big tomorrow," is not bad advice.

Syd Syvertson, wealthy and successful, has a giant real estate organization on the West Coast. He's come up a long way from when he was twenty-two and started selling homes in the Midwest. I was his sales manager.

He had only been at it for two months when he came into my office and said, "I just left a lady. I know she wants this home, but she thinks it's too much money. I was selling as hard as I knew how to sell, and she was resisting to the point where she finally got a headache and asked me to leave."

"Syd, climb in your car and go right back to see her," I advised. "When she comes to the door, smile and apologize for being so persistent. If she'll let you in, sit down, relax, keep smiling, and tell her you were both much too serious. You were trying too hard and she simply got uncomfortable. Laugh a little. Make small talk. If she feels better, more at ease, her resistance will lower."

A few hours later Syd came into the office with an ear-to-ear grin and a signed purchase agreement!

Challenge Resistance

Sometimes resistance can be reduced by standing up face-to-face and defying it by saying, "That's the way things are. If you choose to resist, OK, but it won't change anything."

I first encountered this when a salesman was trying to sell me something and I was hemming and hawing, putting in his way all the little stumbling blocks I could think of.

Finally he just stopped, looked me squarely in the eye, and said, "Mr. Conklin, if you're trying to tell me 'no,' go ahead and say it. I'll stop wasting your time, be on my way, and we'll still be friends. But just say 'no' if that's what you really want to say."

"That's not it at all," I stammered. "I was just thinking as you went along."

I kept my mouth shut and bought. Later I learned he was the top salesperson in his division. His handling of my resistance impressed me as kind of a gutsy approach, but effective.

Maybe you want to muffle it down and use it something like this:

"I think I hear what you're saying. You're against this. And maybe no amount of talking will change your mind. If that's the case, just say so, and we'll visit about something else."

Or, "I know you're dead set against what I'm suggesting. I can't change that. But I want to go ahead with it anyway. It's very important to me."

Or, "If I understand what you're telling me, you don't want anything to do with this idea. If that's so, it means you'll keep us from ever knowing whether or not it will work. It may be the greatest idea since sliced bread. But we'll never find that out if we don't try it. Is that what you want?"

All right. So much for neutralizing resistance by reducing its significance in the other person's thoughts. Let's move on to the third major process for handling resistance.

REMOVING RESISTANCE BY CONVERSION

This one's easy to explain. Simply convert the cause of resistance into a reason for agreement. It takes some imagination and usually preplanning, but it's mighty effective when you can do it.

Scott McKenzie, a crusty old master of the sales profession, was my first sales manager when I began my adult sales career with educational courses. I can still hear his words playing back to me when he'd say, "Anticipate objections and block them out before they ever come up."

I took his advice when I began building direct-sales forces. These were straight commission jobs. Applicants would usually complain that there was no salary, no security, no weekly paycheck.

So I learned to open conversations with, "Perhaps the greatest advantage to this position is that you are compensated by commission. You decide how much you earn. You work as hard as you want to and get paid for every minute you put in. You no longer have others putting ceilings on how much money you make."

Manipulation? Not at all. I said it because I believed it. That doesn't mean it's right for everyone. But for some it puts their income and effort in a perspective of advantage rather than disadvantage.

I've learned that behind every form of resistance there is some advantage, some opportunity, if the situation is studied with positive imagination. It takes some doing, but the effort will help you look at the brighter, positive, possibility side of every indication of resistance.

There are lots of ways you can apply this approach to your encounters.

"I might fail!"

"Well, at least you'd find that out about yourself and go on to something else."

"The price is too high."

"Might seem like it. But it's really a gain. It goes up ten percent in three days."

"What if I don't like it?"

"Well, then you'd know that's one thing you don't like."

"The monthly premiums on that policy are too high."

"That's the best part about it. It's the only way most people can save money. It's a way of paying yourself first. You deserve that!"

"There's no garage with this house."

"Think about that. The house is thirty years old. If a garage had been built then, it would be too small for your car! Now you can put one up any size you want!"

"I don't want to go on the night shift."

"It pays forty-five cents an hour more!"

Whenever you encounter opposition, learn to look behind it for an advantage to the other person.

ACCEPT RESISTANCE

We've gotten into this business of resistance quite heavily. Maybe too much. Because sometimes there's nothing you can do about it. Learn to accept that.

All the people that you've put into your world are distinct individuals, different from each other and you. They want to stay that way. So they will resist people who want to change them. Accepting them as they are is a lot of what friendship is about. These ideas about handling resistance are not designed to give you any special power over others but simply to help your relationships run smoother.

Resistance is a form of pressure. If you can find ways to reduce that on the outside, it'll go down on the inside. You'll be a happier, more peaceful person. Good luck!

14

Must You Be a Doormat?

Must you be walked over, pushed around, and used like a doormat by people? Should you be the one who always gives way to others? Is it necessary to spend the rest of your life catering to the needs, fancies, and whims of those about you in order to get along in this world?

This book would seem to say so, wouldn't it? To the degree you give others what they need, they will give you what you need.

Love. Listen. Give. Be courteous. Ask others to forgive you. Show understanding, tolerance. Don't argue. Make others feel needed, important. Express appreciation.

It almost borders on the bright-sided optimism of Pollyanna, the little girl who saw good in everything and everybody, doesn't it? Perhaps.

But let's consider some alternatives. Like speaking what's on your mind, no matter how it affects others. Get mad. Assert yourself. Fight back. Tell others what you think of them. Be aggressive. Vent your hostilities. Gain power over people. Don't let others get away with anything.

Say what's on your mind even though it's vindictive and hateful.

You can do all those things and more. But I'll tell you what's wrong with them. They don't work. They don't make you like yourself more. They don't attract people to you. In fact, they repel others.

OK. So acting that way makes you feel spunky and bold. The minor frustrations and wrath go away for a while. But over a long period of time your life will fall apart, erode, and you'll be sitting, lonely, alone with your vexations, wondering what went wrong.

I'll give you another possibility. Try setting aside those things that mess up your life. I've been teaching that for years. It's worked for thousands of people. I heard it summed up very neatly once by Terry Cole Whittaker. She's a marvelous speaker and minister of one of the fastest growing churches on the West Coast. Terry said, "If you find something that works in your life, keep it. If something isn't working, let it go."

Isn't that beautiful? It's all so simple. But the difficulty is that people just won't let go of things that don't work. Instead, they spend all their lives struggling to make things work for them that do not have the remotest possibility of making their lives any better.

If you want proof of that, look at the books people are buying, the seminars they're attending, and what drives them to the psychiatrists. It's all about how to handle things that don't work for them.

You can buy books on intimidating others, asserting yourself, how to gain power over those around you, expressing anger, coping with guilt, techniques of selfishness, and a whole array of other such things. But none of those characteristics will make your life function right. They're negative. They get negative results. So why hang on to them, grunting on from day to day, striving to make them work? That's like dousing yourself with perfume when you're hot and sweaty. You might be able to cover up the stickiness and smell, but it won't go away. Soap and water work better.

Let go of whatever it is that's cluttering up your life. You'll discover that your relationships with others will be profoundly improved and you'll like yourself a lot better.

LIKE YOURSELF

Liking yourself. That's so important. The world is a reflection of what you think of yourself. What you see in others is what you see in yourself.

It isn't easy to get high on yourself. The comfortable, secure knowledge that you're what you want yourself to be is hard to come by. Maybe it's because you know what's inside. Ultimately what you think of yourself will be determined by the feedback you get from the world around you.

Other people will do more to make you feel good about yourself than you can ever hope to do alone. Lock yourself in your room, stick out your chest, parade in front of the mirror, tell yourself how great you are. But who are you kidding? Go back out into the world and, if you find it cold and indifferent, all those wonderful thoughts about yourself will crumble away.

But have a stranger smile at you, a boss praise you, an acquaintance ask you over for dinner, a friend treat you kindly, or just one person say, "I love you," and the stock you have in yourself goes up ten thousand points!

You need the positive reinforcement of others to build a healthy self-image. You can't do it alone.

But people are only going to give to you what you give to them.

And you can only give what you've got. If you have love, you'll give love. And that's what you'll get. And you'll feel warm and wonderful about yourself.

On the other hand, if you have hatred, intolerance, resentment, guilt, and anger, that's what you give. And that's what you'll get. How will that make you feel about yourself? Any better?

It's a vicious circle, isn't it? Have hate, get hate. So that causes more hate.

Be angry. Get anger. Judge others. Be judged. My suggestion is to break the circle. Stop fighting to hold on to the stuff that clogs up your relationships with others. Just let it go.

I realize it's not all that simple. But it's not all that complicated, either.

COPING WITH THE BURIED BURDEN OF GUILT

Let's start with guilt.

Little wonder you feel bogged down by the depressing load of guilt at times. The whole order of human relationships revolves about trying to get people to do things by making them feel guilty. Or unloading guilt feelings onto someone else. Or getting revenge by fixing the pain of guilt on an offender.

It starts at an early age.

"Aren't you ashamed of what you've done!" The parent exclaims. What is really meant is, "Don't you feel guilty about yourself!"

The teacher says, "You aren't working up to your potential." And if that doesn't move you, then there's always the possibility of a low grade or even failing. It's a system that's designed to impose shame and guilt on all those except the ones who fall precisely into place. I know the problem; I'm not too sure I know all the solutions. At any rate, it's a gradual process of accumulating guilt.

Wherever you go, whatever you hear, the subtle inference that you're functioning inadequately as a human being is there. Take a greater interest in your government, schools, church, hospitals, elderly, young, or disadvantaged. Eat less, exercise more, work harder, drive slower, be charitable, and love your neighbor, whose dog wakes you up at five every morning.

You're responsible for how your kids turn out, that the marriage partner radiates with delight every moment, and when the payroll gets out each month. Besides, you're polluting the environment, a member of a decadent society, and God's going to punish you real good any moment now for being the awful person you are.

Gets a little heavy, doesn't it? All of it comes out of the minds of people to create guilt and get you to do what they want you to do. The trouble is that you are pulled in so many different directions that you end up just numb and a little lifeless.

REACTING TO GUILT

Guilt. The buried burden of the human soul that takes the joy and freedom from living. Guilt is an unpleasant feeling, and people will do just about anything to get rid of it. If they don't, they end up sick.

During childhood, guilt is disposed of almost automatically. Do something wrong. Get punished. There! It's gone! Now go play and have fun again.

But when you're grown, it's different, isn't it? There's no one around to spank you or send you to your room. So you do all sorts of strange things to punish yourself. Like eating too much or drinking too much. You whip yourself with blame, remorse, and despondency.

Maybe you just make sure you fail at whatever you try to do, whether it's being a parent, salesperson, typist, friend, or spouse. Now you've really chastised yourself, haven't you?

The ultimate sentence, of course, is suicide.

There's another course you may unknowingly follow. Unload your guilt on others. That botches up the identifications with others and gets you nowhere. If you haven't done it, you've seen it.

"It isn't my fault! You made me do it!"

"I ain't workin' as hard as I could 'cause the company ain't treatin' me right!"

There's another outlet for guilt. Use it to make others feel as miserable as you do. Then maybe they'll do something to make you feel better.

"You have no right to act that way!" ("Feel guilty!")

"How come you do those things? When are you going to start

treating me differently?" ("Don't you feel guilty? What are you going to do about me?")

"If you really loved me, you wouldn't talk to me that way." ("Feel guilty. Talk to me in a way that will make me happy.")

"There's no opportunity here. The company has little regard for the employee's future." ("The company should feel guilty. It isn't taking care of me.")

Influencing people by sticking them with guilt feelings won't get you far. There's a better way. Help people feel good about themselves. They'll want you around. That's what this book is about. It doesn't suggest that you use guilt, fear, worry, and ignorance to victimize people into doing what you want them to do.

AVOIDING GUILT

So how about the guilt that others try to lay on you? My wife came up with a good suggestion once on how to handle that.

There was a fellow who was trying to get me to support a business venture in which he was involved. I decided against it. That culminated in a forty-five-minute phone conversation in which he implied I was not being a loyal friend, was letting down a lot of people, and generally was not living up to the standards of responsibilities in business.

I got off the phone, visibly shaken.

My wife had just one brief comment: "Don't let him do that to you!"

It was the best advice I've ever heard on coping with guilt that others try to put on your shoulders. It can be a bloated ballast unless you decide not to accept it.

I've added something to that. It's an affirmation I say when others try to attack me or my life from their dogmatic viewpoint. I say to myself, "I never have to justify or defend who I am, what I've done, or what I believe." And with that I absolutely refuse to allow others to make me feel guilty. It's what works best for me. Try it.

For you can't go through life frantically trying to live up to the expectations of others in every situation. You can't be all things to all people. Only you can decide what kind of a person you want to be.

Of course, if you're not being what you know you ought to be, it's going to be difficult to run away from yourself. No matter how hard you fight it, there's going to be some guilt pangs poking around inside.

There's a way of coping with that kind of guilt that's going around these days. Pretend it isn't there. Do your thing. Ignore what others think.

Go ahead. Have an affair. Everybody's doing it. A couple of current books even recommend it as a way of relieving pressure. After all, the person you're married to should understand that it has nothing to do with the way you feel about him or her.

Use foul language. Tell rotten stories. Read the stuff that's run out of a sewer pipe. It's all right. This is the modern age of letting everything hang out. Nothing wrong with anything today. Be yourself. It's that Victorian morality that got everybody uptight in the first place.

Do unto others whatever you can get away with. If you can abuse, exploit, use, manipulate, and take advantage of them, great! That should be a feather in your hat! Put another scalp on your belt and keep going. If you can do that to people and get away with it, that's their problem, not yours. So why feel guilty?

I'll tell you what's wrong with all that. It won't work.

It begins with you. For imbedded within you is a respect for right and wrong, fairness, and a sensitivity for the feelings of others. There is a fineness, a wonder beyond your understanding, a sense of beauty, an urging to rise to the highest level of the human spirit, and your conscience is always telling you how you're handling that part of you. It won't go away. You can tuck it behind a lot of rationalization, justification, and advice from eggheads who try to salve you with their philosophy of anything goes.

But you know that's not right, don't you? By knowing that, and listening to the little voice called "conscience" talking to you from somewhere around your heart, you set yourself apart as a pretty decent human being. You can feel good about yourself. You've got quality and class. You have a little of why civilization is a lot better off today than it was five thousand years ago.

So I say, "Don't waste a lot of time trying to make guilt work. Just don't do those things that make you feel guilty."

I tell that to people and they say, "That's too simple. It isn't that easy."

Yes, it is. Just stop doing or being whatever makes you feel guilty. Don't hang on to guilt, trying to live with it. There are a lot of people, including yourself, who will try to convince you that's all right. It isn't. It won't work. Ellen Goodman, the columnist, describes it best:*

> I knew a man who went into therapy three years ago because, as he put it, he couldn't live with himself any longer. I didn't blame him. The guy was a bigot, a tyrant and a creep.
>
> In any case, I ran into him again after he'd finished therapy. He was still a bigot, a tyrant and a creep BUT . . . he had learned to live with himself.
>
> I suppose this was an accomplishment of sorts. I mean, nobody else could live with him. But there seem to be an awful lot of people running around and writing around these days encouraging us to feel good about what we should feel terrible about, and to accept in ourselves what we should change.
>
> The only thing they seem to disapprove of is disapproval. The only judgment they make is against being judgmental, and they assure us that we have nothing to feel guilty about except guilt itself.
>
> It seems they are all intent on proving that I'm OK and you're OK, when in fact, I might be perfectly dreadful and you may be unforgivably dreary, and it may be—gasp! WRONG.
>
> They are all Dr. Feelgoods, offering us placebo prescriptions instead of strong medicine. They give us a way to live with ourselves, perhaps, but not a way to live with each other.

Living with each other. There are a lot of people feeling guilty about the way they do that.

Ellen Goodman, the Washington Post Company.

There's the man and wife I knew once who were always chipping away at each other, nagging, criticizing, and piling up put-downs. They pretended they had a good marriage. It wasn't all that rosy. They got sick a lot and didn't act very happy.

I thought they secretly carried around a lot of guilt from making each other feel miserable. They went to seminars and read books that told them to voice their feelings, and if the partner got hurt or angry then it was all a part of letting everything out.

So they became dart boards to each other, and if one could fling a remark that would hit deep, it was a bull's-eye! They harped away with cutting little digs and then gurgled, "Isn't it wonderful how open and honest we are!"

That, to me, was trying to make guilt work for them. It didn't. Their troubles deepened. But why didn't they just stop acting that way and be nice to each other? If they couldn't find something good to say about the other one, then say nothing? If they would have invested as much time trying to make each other happy as they did making each other unhappy, they might have discovered how great being together could be.

I'm acquainted with a businessman who owns a good-sized company and treats his employees terribly. He's demanding, abusive, and totally unreasonable in what he expects of them. He has some tyrannical obsession that is evidently satisfied by his autocratic behavior.

But something is gnawing inside that deprives him of self-satisfaction. It's his guilt. So he spasmodically buys his people expensive gifts or throws a lavish party for them. In a bungling way he's trying to buy his way out of his guilt.

He's going through a heap of frustration and money holding on to guilt, trying to make it fit into his life. If he'd stop doing what makes him feel that way and instead treat his people with consideration, respect, and decency, his life would be a whole lot better.

You can't escape what you know about yourself. If there's something inside that you don't like, there's nothing you can do to feel good about it. You'll get gobs of guilt. That tends to muddy up the way you mix with people.

So why not get rid of guilt—stop doing or being whatever causes it? It probably starts with some meaty advice that's been around for the last few centuries. William Shakespeare wrote it: "This, above all—to thine own self be true/ And it must follow, as the night the day/ Thou canst not then be false to any man."

15

Handling Anger and Hate

I just finished reading a book about anger. It described an assortment of situations that caused anger. Anger, according to the author, is a natural emotion that must be allowed to flow out. It was a sort of "how-to" book on living with anger.

How does that strike you? It seemed rather senseless to me. Because anger isn't natural; it's unnatural. It doesn't make a person any better. Rage, wrath, and ire never worked in anybody's life.

You were not born with anger. You learned it. At one time it got what you wanted.

As a child you cried. If that didn't get attention, you screamed. If there were still no results, you went into a temper tantrum—kicking, squirming, even pounding your head against whatever was available. That usually did it. People did things for you. It took genuine anger and rage to pull that off, but it got people's attention. They did what you wanted, and you felt better.

Now you've grown up. Or have you? Do you still get angry

when you want people to do something to cause you to feel better? The boss isn't doing what should be done so that working is a pleasure. You smolder. "What are you going to do about my job?" you think.

Your marriage partner is currently not loving you with sufficient gestures of adoration. "What are you going to do to make me happy?" are the words burning holes in your mind.

So you stew and fuss and let yourself be upset, groping for the answer to the question that you keep asking of the world, "What are you going to do about my life?"

I'll tell you what the world is going to do about your life. Very little. Life is a do-it-yourself project. That might seem unjust and cruel, but it's reality. You can churn and burn inside until your ears turn crisp, but it won't help.

Some people never come to grips with that. In one of the first sales forces I ever managed I had a salesman who would go into a tirade if anything or anyone would go against him.

It got so that everyone would tiptoe around, not wanting to do anything to upset Mike. That included me. Until I realized what he was doing to me. He had me intimidated by his anger.

So we had a chat. I said I would never again agree to anything he asked me to do when he was angry. We got along fine after that. He stopped using his tantrums as devices to get me to do something.

It was a valuable lesson. Since then I've seen people in organizations who do the same thing. They fume and bluster, and everybody of a milder nature gives in. In fact, in some encounters of controversy it is the person who huffs and puffs and snorts the loudest who is considered to be most right. It's a wacky process for arriving at a decision, but it gets results for some. So they splutter and storm when the chips are going against them.

But eventually these people isolate themselves. They don't get ahead. They become known for their immaturity and others dodge and work around them.

So anger and rage are not long-range tools for getting the cooperation of others. Don't get into the habit of flying off the handle to win people to your side.

That's not to imply that you are never going to get mad. You are. What do you do about it? How does it affect your encounters with others?

HOW DO YOU HANDLE ANGER?

Let's look at the possibilities. Driving a car would be a fit example to use to size up how you might act when angry. Perfectly nice people go into all sorts of emotional gymnastics when they start herding that two tons of metal down a freeway.

For instance, you leave your home in the morning. Before you get to your destination there are drivers who cut you off, honk, go too slow in the left-hand lane, tailgate you, and are driving automobiles that are too big, too noisy, or too old.

No everyday circumstance offers more possibilities for getting irritated than driving a car.

How do you handle your hostility and frustration? Well, you could do something about it, like getting really mad. Don't take it sitting down. Be aggressive, assertive, really let it out and do your thing. Buy an old pickup truck. Have it mounted with enormous wraparound bumpers and roll bars. Install a public address system and air horns. Put neon signs on the front and back with flashing instructions on how to drive.

Then for the rest of your days you can coast along the highways bumping people out of the way, telling them off, and blasting away with your horn when they do something wrong.

You can even stop suddenly in front of the tailgaters, causing them to crash into the back of your truck with no great damage to you, but a ruined front end for them. That would teach them something, wouldn't it? Of course your insurance rates might run rather high, but your annoyance would not remain suppressed. And your life would be dominated and run by your anger. Pretty soon you'd be a mess. You could even get killed that way.

DON'T LET ANGER CONTROL YOU

Here's another idea. Don't get angry in the first place. Stop driving competitively. Relax. Start earlier; take more time. Don't allow others to upset you. Ride along in your own lane, enjoy the radio music, and smile at the people with frowns on their faces.

Every time you try to make anger work in your life, it's like buying that pickup truck. Analyze all the situations that anger you. Avoid them. Figure out what irritates you, and then stop exposing yourself to that sort of torment.

Anger is developed by you. It can get to be a habit if you let it.

I know a young married couple who decided that they were going to set a specific time aside once a week to tell about what each one had done to make the other angry.

"You know what happened?" the woman told me. "We found that we were getting into the habit of being angry at each other. Our marriage was becoming filled with blame, hostility, and keeping track of who made which one the angrier. Popping off about it didn't decrease anger. It increased it. So we started working to get rid of it. That was a turning point for the better."

Is there anything wrong with being gentle and kind? That doesn't seem to be suggested much anymore. Still, it works so much better than fury and temper.

It's not the situation that angers you. It's your reaction to the situation.

It's not the person who angers you. It's your reaction to the person. And the individual who angers you conquers you. You are held in that person's power. Is that what you want?

The most significant cause of your anger toward others is the belief that people are doing terrible things to you. They are threatening you, treating you rudely, ignoring you, or endangering your fragile self-esteem. Maybe that's why you can be angry.

It's a protective emotion; in a rage you become stronger, wilder, more destructive. At one time that might have given some apey guy courage to flail away at a dinosaur, but it doesn't prove much anymore.

What do you do with your anger? If it's the perpetual, simmering, general reaction to what you are or how others treat you that's deep down, then you should deal with it in a logical way. Talk it out. Get counseling. Find out what makes it. But don't work to hang on to it.

If your anger is the spontaneous type, like most people's, that's a different matter. You can brood about it, carry around grudges, and blow it off like a popped balloon.

I tried that once.

My eighteen-year-old daughter told me, "Dad, you never show anger. You must have times when you feel it. But you don't let it out. You turn it back in and bury it. That's not good for you."

I thought about it. Maybe she was right. So the next time something came up that I could get mad about, I did. And I hung it out for everyone to see—tangling up my face, growling, raising the voice, and steaming up inside.

Somehow it didn't fit. For me, it wasn't right. I didn't like myself any better. I felt a little foolish, as if I had lost control. However, I could live with that. What made it wrong was that the coals didn't cool off. They kept on burning, even got hotter.

EMOTIONS ARE SHAPED BY BEHAVIOR

I discovered that when I acted angry, I felt angry. The angrier I acted, the angrier I felt, and the longer it stayed with me. What happened to me was not without professional reinforcement. Years ago Dr. William James, one of the giants of modern psychology, pointed out that you cannot control your emotions by your will. But you can control your *actions* by your will. And when you act a certain way, you feel a certain way.

In other words, if you are going to feel happy, you must act happy. To feel successful, act successful. Life is a laboratory of action and reaction. Your emotions are a reaction to your behavior.

Therefore, if you let yourself act angry, you'll feel angry. That advice of draining off anger by venting it every chance you get doesn't make it go away. Showing it might give you the jollies because you're bold enough to put it up front where everyone can see it. If you need that more than you need friendship, love, faith, confidence, and the respect of others, then keep on blowing your stack. But it's a way of trying awfully hard to make something work that never will.

THERE'S ANOTHER WAY

If you get tired of being alone with your rages (because that's where they will eventually lead you!), then try this. Nip it. Cool it when you feel the stomach tightening, the heart beating faster, and the mind grinding. Walk away from the situation if you have to, but don't self-destruct.

Old Willy James's advice works just as well with positive emotions as it does with negative emotions. Act a certain way, feel a certain way. Get cool and you'll feel cool. And anger will no longer be a dividing factor in your encounters with others.

Best of all, you'll like yourself better. You'll have an aroused awareness that you have something to say about what you are. You're the master, you're in control of you. That's a good feeling.

Remember, I'm not saying that every suggestion in this book is the answer for everybody. That goes for anger. What's right for my daughter may not be right for me. What's OK for Gladys might not be OK for Charlie. Situations vary. What goes well in a corporate boardroom may not be suitable for swinging a machete in the Amazon.

Each person has to learn to deal with emotions in his or her own way. In the end you have to handle anger or hate or guilt in the way that seems to come out best in your life.

Put these ideas to use. If they work, keep them. If they don't drop them. Go on to something else. But keep trying. For you have within you the power to put your life together in such a way that it keeps on going somewhere that's good for you. That's growth.

If you're growing in one area, learning to manage one emotion like anger, you're acquiring the ability to subdue any negative quality. Another biggie is hate.

THE INSIDIOUS EFFECTS OF HATE

I see people in corporations, marriages, churches, and occupational groups straining to gain the confidence and cooperation of others. They attend classes, seminars, and study groups and read all the books they can on human relations and influencing people. Still, they get nowhere. They're on a treadmill for one reason. They hate.

Their hatred may take many forms. It may appear as sarcasm, coldness, indifference, caustic criticism, or prejudice. Of all these, prejudice is perhaps the best disguised. It is probably the outlet for more hatred than any other characteristic of the human being. Prejudice drives more wedges between people than any other single force, inevitably hurting the prejudiced one, mentally and spiritually, more than any other.

Prejudice is caused by ignorance, a closed mind. It is often seen in people who are confused. It is a sign of desperately trying to make some sense out of one's own jumbled thinking. This type of person will belligerently attack another's set of beliefs, hoping it will straighten out the crooked pathways within the person's own mind.

Hanging on to discrimination and prejudice is another instance of individuals trying to make something work in their lives that is woefully harmful to them. Why is this? It is one of the mysterious enigmas of human rationalization.

At the moment of writing this I am just outside the old whaling village of Lahaina on the island of Maui, Hawaii.

I've been reading of the millions of people who visit Hawaii every year. They come from the plains, cities, and every country in the world to spend time on these islands rising from ocean waters. They flock to the tourist attractions—the mountain valleys, waterfalls, beaches, pineapple plantations, and artifacts of the Polynesian culture.

Almost without exception there is a certain sameness about the tourists' reactions. "How different it is from where we come from!" they say.

They find the islands elegantly lovely and the native people gracious and charming. They go back to their homes refreshed and invigorated, saying, "The change did us good!"

They came with inquiring minds and receptive senses and found that change was good for them. Beautiful! But isn't it strange that what human beings see in the world about them they fail to see in each other? That which is different, unique, contrasting, and beyond understanding in nature is found fascinating and stimulating. But those same qualities expressed in another human being become threatening, wrong, and the basis for rejection, scorn, and prejudice.

DIVERSITY COULD BE BENEFICIAL

Often prejudice becomes most treacherous and harmful when it creeps into a supposedly similar-minded group. It is fairly common, for example, for members of a single church group to become viciously separated from one another by small variations of belief or viewpoint. It seems so ridiculous, because an intelligent examination of all the world's great religions would reveal a remarkable similarity in their greater purposes and meanings. Actually, if prejudice could be set aside, individuals would find an enlarged personal growth and spiritual understanding through the study of the various religions, rather than spiteful criticism of other's beliefs.

The same is true of organizations. It is not unusual to see companies and institutions split apart by factions girded by selfish interests and individual opinions. How unfortunate, when each member could benefit so much more by striving to come together, strengthened by the diversities of each other, rather than separated by them.

People need each other for their differences, not their similarities. America has become a great nation because it has worked at doing something no other civilization in history has achieved. People of all different races, cultures, beliefs, and ethnic origins have fought to live together as one nation. They have problems, and the dream has not been fully realized, but progress is being made.

Prejudice among age groups and sexes can be dreadfully limiting. Why do people battle to cling to such traits that are apparently detrimental to them? The young need the old, and the old need the young. Men are helped by women, and women gain from men. Why should there be spite and malice between such individuals?

It is a misconception that only those who are alike belong together. When my wife and I were first married, we were as different as elephants and ants. She was a city girl; I was a small town fellow. She was night; I was morning. One was intellectual, the other emotional. She was a people person; I was more of a loner. She liked beer; I went for milk. We were continents apart in our religious philosophies.

I was devoted to golf, running, and a business career. She was more inclined toward dancing, playing cards, and raising kids. That's for starters. There were many more little idiosyncracies.

But we haven't tried to change each other, only accept and understand the other's differences. Over the years I have become more like her and she more like me in the ways we've chosen to be. We have both enjoyed growth and change because of our dissimilarities. And we still have many of those today. We like it that way. It makes living together an adventure.

Where would we be now if we'd have been exactly alike or prejudiced against the other's unfamiliar characteristics? Probably apart or engulfed in an unhappy marriage. But we aren't. And it's because we have tried to do what is essential to removing any form of hatred imbedded in prejudice. That's being open-minded and intellectually alive.

Those two qualities, openness and a stimulated curiosity for people's wide range of attitudes and behaviors, will dissipate hatred.

To the contrary, a rigid mind becomes imprisoned with its dogmatic prejudices. When an intellect stops inquiring and expanding, it starts dying, drawn lifeless by the parasites of hate and indifference.

SO YOU DON'T LIKE SOMEONE

So much for prejudice. That still leaves the inescapable fact that there are some people who just rub you the wrong way. Try as hard as you might, you find it quite impossible to like them.

That used to bother me about myself. I did my best to "love my enemies" as the Bible dictated. But I couldn't. I was unable to remove from my thoughts how unjustly and wrongly I had been treated by another person. Love was out of the question.

However, in spite of the way I felt, I found I could do something for that person. When I went out of my way to help the individual, my feelings of hostility melted away.

I started teaching that technique in my attitudes and human relations classes. "Help the person who bugs you the most," I suggested. The results were absolutely amazing! Old wounds were healed, hidden aggravations were weeded out, and even family situations became dramatically improved by those who extended simple acts of kindness as a way of warming frigid relationships.

There's a little saying posted in our house now that reads, "Love your enemies. It drives them nuts." It really does. Consideration and helpfulness when it is least expected gets some surprising reactions. People often are doubly anxious to respond in like manner to such treatment.

Try ridding yourself of discord, rivalry, or grudges like that. Look at love more as "doing" than "feeling." See if the doing of love doesn't wash out the feeling of dislike.

It's worth the effort, as this sign on a New York City bus advises:

> Doctors tell us that hating people can cause: ulcers, heart attacks, headaches, skin rashes and asthma. It doesn't make the people you hate feel too good either.

GUILT, ANGER, AND HATE ARE GARBAGE

Guilt, anger, and hate are only three of the emotional nuisances that get in the way of friendly relationships. We all have others. But if we learn to handle this threesome, the rest will come easy.

All these negative attitudes come under a swampy collection titled "junk." It's the clinkers we put in our thinkers.

"Stinkin' thinkin'," some call it—or cranium crud.

"Gigo" is the word they use in the computer trade. That stands for "garbage in, garbage out."

Program your mind with a bunch of garbage, and that's what's going to be experienced in your life, including the associations with other people. What are you putting in up there? Look within yourself. For what gives you displeasure about yourself is generally what disturbs you about others.

The knowledge you have of yourself you use as the knowledge you have of those about you. You look at the world not as it really is, but as you are.

It is incredible how accurately your relationships reflect what you think about yourself. Focus attention on what you aren't, and you'll dwell on what others aren't. You'll be more concerned with their negatives than their positives. This will come out as sour grapes and criticism.

Speak ill of friends, and you'll assume they're doing the same about you.

Know in your heart that you are dishonest, and you will be suspicious of others. Distrust yourself, and you will distrust all.

Consider yourself unlovable, and you'll be insecure in your close associations, constantly demanding that those you care about prove in a number of little ways that they care about you.

So if you want to get along with others, it is vitally important that you first get along with yourself.

It is easy to tell you to do this by not feeling guilty, angry, or prejudiced. But these are natural responses to life situations. You shouldn't feel evil about having them. They are proof that you are a sensitive, feeling human being, responsive to all of life's dimensions.

But to do nothing about the grumpy moods that keep you down is to admit that you have no control over your life. It isn't that you have "junk" (everyone has a certain amount) but what you do with it that counts.

Some try to bag it. It won't stay that way. Someone opens the bag and the junk comes out—anger, hate, put-downs. There are those who just try to stick it away, hide it, where it won't be noticed. Then, pop! Like a jack-in-the-box, the lid comes open and out jumps the debris. Anything, anyone, might open the lid—fatigue, setback, anxiety, tension, bad vibrations, or just rubbish piling up.

DO SOMETHING ABOUT NEGATIVE ATTITUDES

So how do you cope? How do you handle your "junk"? Well, you work at it. You try to manage it. You learn to process it in as short and harmless a period as possible. You stop hanging on and justifying the stuff that isn't working for you. Just do something.

Do anything, but do something. Take a walk, kick a tree, go shopping, pray, play solitaire, or whatever strikes your fancy. Be good to yourself by doing something you like to do or that drains off the fired-up emotion. Keep doing it until you feel better. Then deal logically with the situation that ticked you off.

Here are some thoughts that might prove helpful as you do that.

1. Know that it'll go away. As long as you're doing something, you're healing.

2. If you let it out, don't be self-destructive. Don't say or do a lot of things that you'll regret.

3. Don't blame yourself. Your emotions are not you. And emotions can be pretty stupid sometimes. Talking about your dumb old emotions might help.

4. Don't blame others. It doesn't work for you. You're responsible for how you feel, not others.

5. You're also responsible for a lot of the ways others treat you. You act; people react. It's a fact of life. Don't let your "junk" cause you to get a lot of bad reactions. Keep in control.

6. Stay away from whatever causes bedlam in your belfry that you can't handle. Don't let freaked-out "friends," drugs, booze, and harassment make an idiot trip out of your life.

7. Why be the only one in the world who is so serious about you? Let up. Learn to laugh at what's going on, especially inside you.

8. Tell others about your trouble spots. You'll realize you're not alone. Some answers are bound to surface.

9. If it gets too heavy, get help. Or go to the zoo and scream at the lizards. Dig a hole and fill it back up. Do something violent, crazy, absolutely mad—and harmless.

Keep plugging away. Put yourself in charge of you. You'll probably find that the more thought and effort you spend sensibly ridding yourself of "junk" the more you'll be in control of who you are and where you're going with that precious life of yours.

That's maturity.

16

As Ye Think, So Shall Ye Relate!

The sun was pushing its way up over Diamond Head.

Human heads and surfboards were bobbing between the waves offshore.

Another exotic day was beginning in Hawaii.

On the veranda of the hotel overlooking the sea I was enjoying breakfast with my friend Sakan Yanagidaira, an accomplished young Japanese businessman. We were discussing the marketing of our program, "Adventures in Attitudes," in Japan.

"I am beginning the translation," he said. "I have the names of sixty translators. Out of these I will select three and start them working. We should have it done in six months."

This would cost him money. I asked him, "Would you feel more comfortable if we had a contract, something in writing, between us?"

He thought for a moment and then said, "We use very few contracts in Japan. We risk not even talking of our business dealings. We have the Japanese word *haragei*, which describes the spirit with which we do business in Japan. *Haragei* is a quality that the very successful Japanese businessman has developed almost to a perfection. It is the ability to judge what the other person expects of you."

This was a refreshingly different concept of business relationships than I had known before.

I asked Sakan to continue.

"*Haragei* comes from the word *hara*, meaning 'stomach,' and *gei*, meaning 'art.' It would be the closest word we have to the English word of *empathy*," he explained.

Empathy. Being able to feel as the other person feels.

Haragei. The art of getting within the other person.

I was beginning to understand.

"It must go further than just being able to evaluate the other person's expectations of you," I suggested.

"Yes," he replied. "When we judge the other person's expectations, then we must fulfill them. That is the highest form of business relationship in Japan. It is a lower form of communication if our relationship or expectations must be written down or expressed orally."

I had to think about that for a while. It was so different from what I had been exposed to. In fact, by coincidence, a few days before I had read a card in an airport gift shop that started out saying, "I was not born to live up to your expectations. . . ." Hmmmm——

Other words came to mind:

"That's not my department."

"No one told me to do it."

"That's his job, not mine."

"I don't have to; it wasn't in writing."

"How do I do this job?"

"I'll get going as soon as someone tells me what I'm supposed to do."

"It wasn't in the contract."

EXPECTATIONS TEND TO BE SELF-FULFILLING

After mulling it over, I decided that the western world

operates somewhat the same way as Japan, only not as clear cut and conspicuously. Perhaps because of cultural differences, expectations are resisted more. But they do have a powerful effect on people's behavior.

That was noted in Greek mythology, when a sculptor named Pygmalion carved a statue in ivory of a beautiful woman. He fell in love with his own creation, and Venus gave life to the statue.

The myth inspired George Bernard Shaw's play *Pygmalion*, a story of how Professor Henry Higgins turned a Cockney flower girl into an elegant lady, using language rather than love. The play subsequently became the musical hit *My Fair Lady*.

Psychologists have concluded that the concept is more than fantasy and that one person's expectations can influence the behavior of another. The phenomenon has come to be called "self-fulfilling prophecy"; people become what is prophesied for them.

STUDIES SHOW EXPECTATIONS INFLUENCE OTHERS

For some time it has been accepted that the physician's positive expectations seem to implement the patient's recovery.

Some random studies done by psychologists indicate that the results of children's IQ tests could be affected by the expectations of those administering the tests. Even animals, some experiments showed, responded to people's expectations.

The entire range of expectations and self-fulfilling prophecies was examined in the mid-1960s, beginning with a controversial study of teachers' expectations of students. The children in eighteen classrooms were given a test disguised to supposedly predict "intellectual blooming."

After the test twenty percent of the children were selected at random and their names given to the teachers with the assurances that these children could be expected to show remarkable gains during the coming year. The only differences between the twenty percent and the other eighty percent of the children were solely in the teachers' minds.

Eight months later all the children were retested. It was found that those children identified as most likely to "bloom" did show an excess in overall IQ gain over the others. It was assumed that because the teachers *expected* some students to do better, they did, in fact, fulfill those expectations.

A book was written about teachers' expectations in the classroom. Differences in professional opinions were aroused, and in the next few years nearly 250 studies were done with all sorts of subjects and situations—in schools, factories, banks, offices, sales groups, and even athletic groups. Of these about a third indicated that one person's expectations can influence the behavior of another.

Examples such as the following were given as supportive evidence of the power of expectations.

The agents of a large national insurance agency in New York City were placed in sales groups according to their abilities. The top agents were grouped under the best manager, the average producers were placed under the average manager, and the lowest producers worked with the least able manager. The result was that the top agents far surpassed their previous performance levels and the goals that had been set for them. It was assumed that this was because they were "expected" to achieve superior results.

A study of a group of college graduates in American Telephone and Telegraph concluded that the managerial success of these individuals depended largely on the company's expectations of them.

Half of the swimming instructors in a summer camp were led to believe that their students, girls and boys ages seven to fourteen, were a "high potential" group. Their students became better swimmers than the regular group.

The supervisors of nurses' aides and trainees in machine operations and electronic parts assembly were given the names of several of the workers who showed a special potential for the job. Actually the names were chosen at random. It was found that in most cases the workers designated as having the most ability did much better than the others, with the exception of the female workers and the nurses' aides, who showed no significant difference.

A study in a large number of banks indicated that the managers .whose lending authority was reduced because of high rates of loss became progressively less effective. This resulted in a loss of business to the banks. In an effort to redeem themselves, these managers struggled for loans, accepting some on marginal credit, which proved to be costly for the banks. Thus, it was pointed out that they did what their supervisors expected of them. Their supervisors' expectations became self-fulfilling prophecies.

In the United States Air Force Academy one hundred cadets were randomly assigned to five math classes. The teachers were told the students were divided according to levels of ability. Those in the high-ability classes improved their math substantially.

Another study indicated that perhaps juveniles using drugs had fulfilled the prophecies of their parents' subconscious expectations.

The studies go on and on. But the implications are quite obvious and perhaps a bit frightening—a little like voodoo or the witch doctor poking pins in the doll likeness of an individual and that individual suffering severe anguish, even death. To carry this idea to its ultimate conclusion, one might imagine that all sorts of expectations, positive and negative, may be conjured in the mind of one to create the cauldron of human behavior for another.

OTHER FACTORS SHOULD BE CONSIDERED

Let's examine these examples and studies more closely, for there are characteristics other than expectations or self-fulfilling prophecies that play a part. They are a little like the case of the young boy stealing food. He was examined by psychologists, tested, environmental characteristics noted, and a childhood work-up completed to determine why he stole. Then the arresting officer's report was read, and in it was the sentence that revealed the strongest motivation. It said, "The boy was hungry."

Of course positive expectations of one person are a factor in influencing another's behavior. But to say that expectations alone shape behavior is similar to finding that all professional tennis players have strong wrists and presuming, therefore, that everyone with strong wrists is a superb tennis player. There are a lot of other factors involved with the people in the studies other than mere expectations.

Science, statistics, and studies are wonderful, but sometimes they are little more than verifications of obvious truths.

We know, for example, that people do better with praise, encouragement, and expressed confidence than they do with humiliation, impatience, and indifference.

If human beings are perceived as potentials rather than problems, as possessing strengths instead of weaknesses, as unlimited rather than dull and unresponsive, then they thrive and grow to their capabilities.

Teaching is loving. It is trust and respect. In the studies made the teachers were told, "These students need you. They will respond to you positively, more so than most others."

Compare the attitudes of the teachers in these cases to attitudes of doubt, indifference, or even hopelessness.

The parent who communicates love and trust to the son or daughter is bound to get a different result than the parent who is consumed by fear that the juvenile is going to get involved with drugs or other delinquent behavior. Managers, teachers, physicians, and parents often are communicating most when they believe they are communicating least. Doubt, impatience, despair, and apathy are communicated by evasive glances, silence, and cold tones. This is the kind of atmosphere that suppresses learning.

People look at others in much the same way they look at themselves. They like others if they like themselves. They have confidence in others if they have confidence in themselves. The teachers and managers in the studies were simply expressing this truth. Teachers were communicating to the students the confidence in themselves. The managers were influencing their subordinates by their conception of how they themselves were able to select, train, and motivate the subordinates. Because the teachers were led to believe they could excel, they communicated that belief to the learners.

It's fair, I believe, to conclude that these ideas about expectations indicate the influence that attitudes have in human relations. That's important for you to remember in dealing with others.

YOU ARE ALWAYS COMMUNICATING YOUR THOUGHTS

You are always telling people what you think about them! Your gestures, facial expressions, and tones of voice give your thoughts away. At times this is quite obvious, as it was with the couple who were in their new home for the first day. Most of the cooking utensils were still packed, and the woman needed a pan to warm some food.

"Look, honey," she said to her husband, "will you go over to the neighbors and see if you can borrow a saucepan?"

"Sure," he replied. "Be right back."

But as soon as he got out the door, he began thinking. Here we are, the first day in the neighborhood, and we start off borrowing. What will the neighbors think? Probably take us for a couple of freeloaders. Take the first step with a saucepan, then it'll be a lawnmower, and end up with a TV. Easier to turn down a request for a saucepan than to put up with handouts every day.

The fantasies mounted until the new resident was convinced he was going to get a door slammed in his face by the time he reached the neighbor's house. So he rang the doorbell, and when the fellow came to the door, our hero blurted out, "OK. You can just keep your crummy saucepan! We don't need it anyway!"

The ways attitudes are expressed are usually more subtle than that, but they will come out some way. People don't realize that.

They vainly attempt to conceal what is on their minds and only become more obvious in the process. It is almost impossible to mask your thoughts and feelings from others.

For instance, your children have been bugging you; they have gotten on your nerves. You know you shouldn't feel that way. So you try to cover up. But they know.

Or you're still upset about the argument you had with your mate last Tuesday; there are a few things that have come to mind that you wished you would have said. However, you're trying to act nice because you don't want any more hassle. But you might as well unload; the other one knows "something is wrong."

Then there's Lester in the vegetable department, who has been goofing off lately. It's nothing you can pin down, but unless he shapes up you're going to have to do something. You decide to sit back and see what happens. What's going to happen is nothing. Because you don't feel good about Lester and Lester doesn't feel good about the way you feel about Lester. That's a busy way of saying there's a chill in the air between you two and both of you realize it.

Or you're a rookie salesperson on your first call. You have walked around the block five times, trying to build up courage to go in the front door of that ominous building and talk to the executive who buys what you have to sell. You sense the receptionist is going to grind you up in a pencil sharpener and use you for sweeping compound.

You finally make eye-to-eye contact and find out you were wrong. You're treated quite cordially. After a few minutes' wait you're ushered into a paneled office. There she sits behind the big desk and manicured piles of papers.

Your mouth is full of mush, and there's a jackhammer pounding away where your heart is supposed to be. You might as well break down and confess you're on your first day. She knows. Because you are telling her in dozens of little ways in a language that is not quite definable. They call it body language, kinesics, or body talk. It's the way you communicate nonverbally. The behavioral scientists have been playing around for some time, trying to figure out all the subtle veiled ways human beings act out their hidden thoughts and feelings.

What has been uncovered so far is fairly commonsense stuff. If you scowl, you have something heavy on your mind. Or when you sit with the arms folded and legs crossed you are being defensive, or apt to be resisting. Drumming your fingers and wiggling your foot are signals of impatience.

The researchers will never unravel all the mysterious ways that people broadcast that which they feel within. There are too many variables, too many complex patterns. Fortunately, you do not have to wait for future laboratory research or serve an internship as a psychologist to relate with others at all levels of communication. Your intuition will get you by quite nicely, providing you care, are interested in people, sensitive to them, and are aware of the fact that people often communicate the most when they think they are communicating the least.

So people are always reacting positively, negatively, or indifferently to your secluded attitudes. It's an awesome insight to know that your relationships with others are molded by your thoughts. But wonderful in a way. For if the flavor of your mind is mean, greedy, caustic, or hateful, you will drive others away.

If, on the other hand, you have respect, concern, and a heartfelt feeling for others, then that will be communicated almost as distinctly as the temperature or perfume in the air. Your relationships will be positive. Besides, you'll feel better about you.

LIFE IS THOUGHT

What is being said here is little more than duplication of the wisdom of sages and philosophers for thousands of years. "To think is to live," Cicero explained.

"Your life is what your thoughts make it," Marcus Aurelius

advised. Your life is an extension of your thoughts. Change your thoughts, and life will change! That certainly includes relationships you have with others.

Realizing the importance of attitudes in human relations, I put together a simple little course I called "Adventures in Attitudes" back in 1957. I began teaching it as an evening program in our public schools. It took hold, grew, and, after years of continued development, is now being conducted by thousands of trained coordinators in colleges, companies, churches, governments, hospitals, and public groups throughout the world.

HOW ATTITUDES ARE FORMED

One of the program's strong appeals is that it helps people get along better with others.

"Now you tell me!" you might say. "I've waded through all the suggestions about ways of working with others and now you say it's not what I do, it's what I think! Why didn't you write a book about attitudes, if that's how it's done?"

It's a good question. But there's a strange quality about attitudes. You don't develop them by sitting in your living room reading about them. Nor do you do it by perching cross-legged, musing from dawn till dusk on the grander strains of thinking. Maybe a few do it that way. But not many.

Most people are struggling along in jobs, with families, and in a lot of activities with people, trying to make the best of their lives. They know the importance of thinking, but anger, discouragement, envy, self-concern, and anxieties creep in from time to time. When thoughts like those take over, it's not easy to make them go away.

So how does a person change his or her attitude? It takes practice—thinking and doing together. This book was written with that concept in mind. Practice the ideas written about here. You'll get positive vibrations from the involvements with others. You'll feel good about that. Your life will go better. You'll be more optimistic, sure of yourself, and pleased with those about you.

So what have you done? You've gotten some fresh new attitudes and an improved way of thinking because you've acted differently. It's impossible to separate the two. Thoughts and actions, attitude and behavior, go together. Change one and the other changes. In human relations, however, it is usually easier to change actions than it is thoughts.

GOOD THOUGHTS MEAN GOOD RELATIONSHIPS

So this has been a book about doing things that will help you be more effective in relating to people. But everything suggested flows from the right attitudes.

Be a good listener. Show understanding. Make people feel important. Be tolerant. Handle resistance with patience, harmony, and reason. Let others be themselves. Give of yourself.

Those are the patterns woven into the words of this book. They all require a certain way of thinking, don't they? All represent positive attitudes toward yourself, people, and the life you're living.

There are some *don't's*, too. Don't be manipulative or attempt to exert psychic brutality or domination over others. Don't expect to put together a batch of verbal tricks that will give you power over others.

Don't try to impress others; let them impress you. Gracious sakes! How important that is! We all have within us a little purple person with a toothy grin and a jagged spear jabbing our egos to speak up and get everyone's head turned in our direction.

At the same time we know what we think of the person who gloats, "Oh, how wonderful that you spent three days at Bug Bite Haven on Mud Lake! It's so nice to get away! We just got back from two weeks in Acapulco!"

There are those who are always trying to top others, feeding their egos with the crumbs of their own contrivance. What a pity that their needs will never be pacified. For they come forth as bores. People resent them, reacting with antagonism and dislike.

The best way to favorably impress others is to let them impress you! That's giving them what they need, putting the ideas to work in this book.

There's that word again—*giving*. You can only give away what you have. That's especially true with your inner characteristics such as love and understanding. Those are thoughts and feelings nourished and grown in your own heart and mind, aren't they?

One way of growing them is by giving them. Because then they come back to you in ever increasing abundance. Wonderful system, isn't it?

And that starts another chapter. It's one about expressing and living the ideas we've thought about here. If we both do that, we'll never be apart.

For what we do for others we do for you and me. That's the larger meaning of love.

In what better way can it be summed up than to end the book the same way it started?

"To the degree you give others what they need, they will give you what you need!"